Get More from Your Book and Help Your Fellow Veterans

Veteran Transition Publishing will donate a portion of the proceeds from the purchase of this book to one of the Veterans organizations listed below. To participate:

ISBN

1) Cut out and complete the form below

2) Mail the form and the ISBN from the back book to the address shown on the form.

3) Veteran Transition Publishing will donate a portion of the purchase price to your selected organization.

DONATION FORM

Yes, please contribute a portion of my book purchase price to: **(choose one ✔)**

☐

THE CHEZ FAMILY FOUNDATION
CENTER FOR **WOUNDED VETERANS**
IN HIGHER EDUCATION

Advancing what the University of Illinois campus has done throughout its storied history in disability, The Chez Family Foundation Center for Wounded Veterans will be a source of transformative educational innovations, research breakthroughs, best practice models, and product developments that support student veterans' health, scholarship, and full participation in society. Our vision is to empower disabled student veterans and their families to realize their potential through a world-class education experience that prepares them to lead fulfilling, meaningful, and maximally independent lives.
www.woundedvetcenter.ahs.illinois.edu

☐

Honoring the Path
of the Warrior
HELPING VETERANS FIND A PATH TO PEACE

Honoring the Path of the Warrior provides returning veterans a safe environment and enables them to rediscover meaning, purpose, and joy in their lives through mindfulness, meditation, and community. We offer programs that combine nature, engaging physical activities and mindfulness practices that have been scientifically shown to reduce trauma, depression, anxiety and other conditions related to Post Traumatic Stress. Through participating in our no-cost programs, veterans are able to use their own strengths and experiences to create new, meaningful and productive paths in civilian life.
www.honoringthepath.org

☐

//AVA
IRAQ AND AFGHANISTAN
VETERANS OF AMERICA

Iraq and Afghanistan Veterans of America (IAVA) strives to build an empowered generation of veterans who provide sustainable leadership for our country and their local communities. We work toward this vision by supporting new veterans through programs in four key impact areas: health, education, employment, and building a lasting community for vets and their families.
www.iava.org

Mail completed form and ISBN from this book to:
Veteran Transition Publishing , Attn: Veterans Donation Program, PO Box 11205, Bainbridge Island, WA 98110

Toll Free: 877-569-9816 • Email: Info@VeteranTransitionPublishing.com
www.VeteranTransitionPublishing.com

VETERAN TRANSITION
PUBLISHING

Life During College

The Veteran's Guide to Success

First Edition

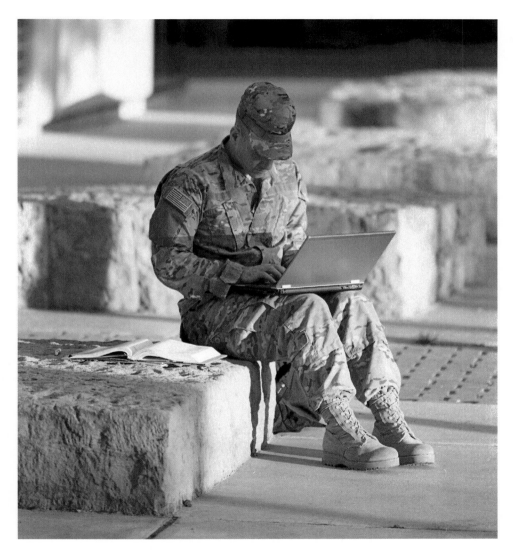

By Dr. Nicholas J. Osborne, Terry Arndt, and Kirrin Coleman

Copyright Information

First Edition, Copyrighted February 2015

Copyright © 2015 Veteran Transition Publishing. All rights reserved. No part of this book, including cover design and websites (www.VeteranTransitionPublishing.com., www.CollegeTransitionPublishing.com, and www.LifeDuringCollege.com), may be reproduced or transmitted in any form, by any means (electronic, photocopying, recording, or otherwise) without the prior written permission from Veteran Transition Publishing. Printed in the United States of America.

Book Disclaimer

Veteran Transition Publishing has made its best efforts in preparing this book to be accurate and complete. The content of the book is not guaranteed to produce any particular results. In addition, the advice given in the book may not suit every individual's circumstances.

Therefore, Veteran Transition Publishing does not assume responsibility for advice given. As a result, each reader should consider their own circumstances and abilities and weigh them versus the advice given.

Veteran Transition Publishing is not in the business of rendering financial, legal, or any professional advice. If any questions regarding financial or legal advice should arise, the reader should seek professional assistance.

Veteran Transition Publishing shall not be held liable for any damages arising from the book's content.

About the Authors

Dr. Nicholas J. Osborne

Nicholas Osborne is the Interim Director of the Center for Wounded Veterans in Higher Education at the University of Illinois at Urbana-Champaign. He is a veteran of the Coast Guard and a former intelligence and law enforcement officer. He completed his Doctorate in Educational Leadership and Administration at the University of California at Davis. He has published numerous peer-reviewed articles, a textbook, and continues to speak at regional and national conferences on topics related to veterans and higher education.

Kirrin Coleman

Kirrin has a Master of Arts in Education from Wake Forest University. She is a National Board Certified teacher who teaches English on Bainbridge Island, Washington. She is the coauthor and editor of
Life During College, Life During College-The Veteran's Guide to Success, Life During Community College, Life During College-The Online Learner's Guide to Success, Life After Graduation, Backpack to Briefcase, and
Camo to Career.

Terry Arndt

Terry earned his Master of Business from the University of Florida. During his education, he found that sharing information with his classmates on how to achieve financial, career and academic success was extremely rewarding. As a result of his passion for helping others, Terry developed and launched College Transition Publishing during his MBA program. Since 1999, Terry has authored and published 15 publications, written numerous papers, and presented on hundreds of college campuses to tens of thousands of college students about achieving success during the college transition process. Terry is currently the President of Veteran Transition Publishing, a division of College Transition Publishing (www.VeteranTransitionPublishing.com and www.CollegeTransitionPublishing.com).

Acknowledgments

The transition out of the military to college is an exciting and formative step for many veterans. It is, most accurately, a process with many complex parts. To create a resource that accurately speaks to veterans and that provides comprehensive support for their unique needs requires the assistance of many talented individuals. Based on this, the authors would like to acknowledge and thank the following reviewers for their insightful suggestions regarding the development of this work.

Tawnya L. Beermann, M.A.
Associate Dean of Completion
Western Iowa Tech Community
College
Sioux City, IA

Michael W. Carrell, Colonel,
USAF (Ret)
Assistant Provost and Director of
Military and Veterans Services
The Ohio State University
Columbus, OH

Jean Driscoll
8-time Boston Marathon
Champion & Olympic Hall of Fame
University of Illinois at
Urbana-Champaign
Champaign, IL

Rodrigo Garcia, MBA, MPP
Chairman, Board of Directors
Student Veterans of America
U.S. Marine Veteran

Karen Hauschild
Director, Academic Advising
and Planning Center
College of Charleston
Charleston, SC

Lolly Hemphill
Academic Advisor, Academic
Advising and Planning Center
College of Charleston
Charleston, SC

Louis F. McIntyre, Sr.
Chair, Math & Science Department
Robeson Community College
Lumberton, NC

Wendy Rasmussen
Ensign, Medical Service Corps,
U.S. Navy Reserve
Doctoral Candidate,
Counseling Psychology
University of Iowa
Iowa City, IA

Jamie M. Richards
Senior Assistant Director
Military Veteran and
Nontraditional Student Programs
Purdue University
West Lafayette, IN

Wendy Stephens
Academic Advisor, Academic
Advising and Planning Center
College of Charleston
Charleston, SC

Geri E. Young, LCSW
Technical Sergeant, Air National Guard
Former Vice President, Illinois
Veterans Student Organization
University of Illinois at
Urbana-Champaign, Champaign, IL

Jump Start Your College Success

Right Now ✔

- [ ] Navigate the Veterans Office website at your college. Become familiar with the types of services and resources available to veterans.

- [ ] Locate the Financial Aid Office and identify contact information for the Veterans Certifying Official.

- [ ] Schedule a time in the next 24 hours to tour the Athletic Center.

- [ ] Check out the Tutoring Center and Writing Lab: Where are they? What services do they offer? What are their hours?

- [ ] Write down 3 goals for today, 3 goals for this week, and 3 goals for this month. Post your goals where you can see them.

This Week ✔

- [ ] Connect with another student veteran. This may happen at a Student Veterans Lounge or by emailing the Student Veterans of America Chapter at your college.

- [ ] Locate the nearest Department of Veterans Affairs (VA) medical clinic or Vet Center. Get registered and become familiar with the types of services and resources they provide.

- [ ] Sit near the front in your classes.

- [ ] Review class notes at the end of each day.

- [ ] Complete the **Personal Study Conditions Inventory** in Chapter 9 on *p. 77,* then create a study plan.

Table of Contents

CONTENTS

The Lay of the Land

Your Academic Life

You, the College Student

Your Money

Your Career

Sources

Military & College Life

CHAPTER 1

Reflecting back to the bus ride to boot camp or basic training, you probably had a lot of thoughts race through your mind like, "What am I getting myself into?" or "Is this the right decision?" Maybe these thoughts included images of impossible obstacle courses or seething drill instructors hovering over your bunk at zero dark thirty while yelling through a bullhorn. Regardless of your branch of service, the quiet hours that took place on the bus before all the noise and chaos were likely filled with mixed feelings that ranged from excitement and anticipation to downright fear and doubt. Now, as you make the transition from service member to student, you may encounter similar feelings.

As a veteran, you're not a stranger to transition and the ability to adapt and overcome. Throughout your military career, you not only received training and developed expertise from the finest military in the world, you also endured deployments, separation from loved ones, and a move every couple of years. Although these experiences have no doubt given you an edge, the transition process is still a complex undertaking and will vary depending on whether or not you are a first-termer, retiree, active duty member, or if you're currently affiliated with the Reserves or National Guard.

Upon leaving the military, most service members participate in the Transition Assistance Program (TAP). TAP classes often consist of a comprehensive three-day workshop that provides an abundance of information ranging from job search strategies to VA benefits. While helpful, many veterans have remarked that their TAP experiences were overwhelming, due to the sheer volume of information presented, and did not provide enough specific information about attending college.

To assist with your transition to college, this book was written with you, the veteran, in mind. College is an adventure that goes beyond academics. As a veteran you value taking risks and having a mission, which makes you an ideal candidate for this new task. The rewards of higher education are many and your veteran status already proves your capacity to charge forward. So, be fearless, be open and, most importantly, enjoy the adventure!

This chapter will discuss the following topics:

- Military culture and college culture
- What it means to attend college as a veteran
- Student veteran strengths, as well as pitfalls to watch out for

Military Culture and College Culture

Generally speaking, core aspects of military culture include

- discipline
- organized hierarchy and rank system
- communication that is direct and to the point
- irregular work hours and a possibility of hazardous conditions
- an emphasis on teamwork, not individualism
- not talking about your problems ("Suck it up and drive on…")

Veterans arrive at college after having spent a good portion of time living and working within a unique culture. Not only is there a military alphabet and dictionary of acronyms, there is also a military culture, which can be characterized as a highly structured setting with its own customs and policies. Some veterans discuss the military as a "different world" when compared to civilian society. While on campus, you are likely to experience these differences in culture.

From those early days in training you were taught to get up early, fold your clothes so they were inspection ready, engage in physical activity, and work as part of a team. In short, you learned to move beyond your individual desires and interests in order to serve a larger good and accomplish your mission. Even learning in the military is different in the sense that training and education focuses on practical application rather than theory. Moreover, military education often takes place as a group activity with all students being on the same regimented schedule with a swift accountability system of consequences for being late or absent.

In college, however, education is more self-directed: you attend class on your own and are responsible for creating your own study schedule. Missing class or arriving late won't necessarily be met with scorn. In fact, it might not even be noticed, particularly in large lecture halls. Additionally, most students take multiple classes during a quarter or semester, which means they must prioritize their time. Developing sound time management and study skills is paramount for being a successful student and will be discussed at various intervals in the coming chapters.

Attending College as a Veteran

Whether you have decided to get additional training for a specific career or you seek personal enrichment and knowledge, there is a *reason* you have decided to go to college. As a veteran, you are a nontraditional learner which means you are different from many of your 17- and 18-year-old peers who recently finished high school and lived at home with their parents. Although you may not be much older than your classmates, the disparities in your life experiences and the things you did in the military will likely set you apart. Also, because you had a break from education due to your military service, it is very common to feel uncertain or anxious about being a student, particularly when thinking about math or writing papers.

Veterans differ from traditional students in the following ways:

- Veterans are often older

- Veterans are more likely to have at least one dependent, such as a spouse or child, while going to school

- Veterans are more likely to commute to campus and to be less involved in campus-based activities

- Veterans often work while attending school

- Veterans are more likely to have a documented disability

- Veterans often report feeling "rusty" when going back to school

Student Veteran Strengths

Consider This ...

> Now that I'm a student I'm concerned about a lot of things, like remembering how to study for a test since I've been out of school for a long time. I'm also worried that I won't relate to my classmates because I'm older and have already had a career.
>
> **Chris, Marine Corps Veteran**

Veterans are unlikely to be homesick and are comfortable working in diverse environments. Unlike your civilian peers, you have likely spent a good bit of time living in various locations throughout the country or abroad. Many veterans have also worked and served within a diverse workforce with people from a broad range of ethnic, cultural and socioeconomic backgrounds.

Veterans are disciplined and reliable. From getting up early for physical training to working long and irregular hours, veterans know what it means to be on time and to stay on task until the job is completed.

Veterans are hard working. Many veterans joke that a 40-hour work week is an easy week. Veterans know the importance of paying attention to detail and of doing things in the exact manner in which they've been trained.

Veterans know how to adapt. Structured deployment training cycles, being in the field or on watch, and sleeping in cramped or dangerous places—veterans know how to adapt to their environment.

Veterans are resourceful. Veterans know how to make do with less. From being sleep deprived and hungry to having the wrong tools for the mission, veterans know how to be resourceful and meet their objectives.

Veterans are mature. From an infantry squad leader to a boat driver on a search and rescue mission, the military demands its members take their jobs seriously. Although many veterans attend school in their 20s and 30s, their unique life experiences have matured them.

Pitfalls to Watch Out For

Too much, too soon. The culture of the military expects you to learn quickly so you can assist your team. This often means putting in long hours to study, train and prepare for the mission. One of the biggest pitfalls veterans encounter, particularly in their first year of college, is the "too much, too soon" syndrome. For example, a veteran might enroll in too many credit hours or in a course sequence that is disproportionately challenging (e.g., all math and science courses) or he or she might "cram" a bunch of material into a short period of time, such as studying the night before an exam without preparing beforehand.

Isolating. You may find that it is hard to relate to your younger classmates or because you commute to campus it may be challenging to get involved in different activities. Although many veterans treat college like a job, it is important to blend your academics with other interests and not to isolate yourself. A student veteran organization can be a great way to meet similar peers and engage in a variety of social and service-based activities.

Not knowing what resources are available. Remember feeling a bit disoriented when reporting to your first unit? Similarly, your college is a vast environment with different types of offices and resources. Take the time to learn about the different support services available.

Not asking for help. Military culture often shuns asking for help. Many veterans feel pressure to not "burden" people when they need help but it is inevitable that at some point in your college career you will need guidance. Don't think of this as a burden but rather think of it as getting the resources you need to accomplish your mission.

Neglecting self-care. You know how to study for hours without a break, skip meals and keep charging, but at some point you will hit a wall. To prevent burnout be sure to incorporate fun and fitness into your routine.

Veterans bring a wealth of experience and knowledge to higher education. They have developed the discipline and warrior mindset that allows them to adapt to their immediate environment and they are competent at putting in the hours and dedication that result in positive outcomes. However, even super-heroes have their vulnerabilities and areas for growth. For veterans, feeling a bit out of place or rusty is a very normal part of the transitional process as is trying to muscle through without assistance. Developing a positive routine early on and identifying helpful resources are paramount for success and will be discussed throughout the next chapters.

College &
Community Resources

CHAPTER 2

You have applied and made it through the waiting game to find out that you're in. As you pack up your boots and BDUs and update your civilian wardrobe you will likely wonder, who are my go-to people on campus and within the community? College is an adventure but as you learned in the military you can't do it alone. You now have a team to help you learn, succeed, stay healthy, meet new people, and even figure out how to pay for the whole experience. The resources available to you are astounding and this chapter will introduce you to some of them. (Note that your school might have different names for some of the resources highlighted below.)

General Support

Dean of Students
The Dean of Students Office serves as the liaison between students and the faculty and administration of the college. Its purpose is to provide a variety of programs and services that support the campus community. The Dean of Students usually coordinates or oversees student activities, student government, and campus safety. This office—or its website—is a great starting place for learning more about campus life. It's also the go-to resource if you have a question and you're not sure where to direct it.

Disability Support Services
For wounded and injured veterans, an acquired disability is a new experience. Disability Support Services offers academic and other important support to students with a range of disabilities and learning differences. It determines eligibility, informs students of their rights, facilitates academic accommodations, works with other campus offices to ensure accessibility, and provides education about disability management and self-care.

It is important for a student veteran to know that campus-based disability services are not tied to the military or Department of Veterans Affairs in any way. For example, a veteran may have a disability rating with the VA, but this information will only be available to a campus disability office if the student veteran authorizes it. Conversely, utilizing disability services on campus will not in any way impact their VA rating or result in additional financial compensation. They are two separate "worlds" and will not share information without the written consent of the veteran.

So, what are the advantages of using a campus disability office? Many veterans find that they experience anxiety before a test or that they need to take exams in environments that minimize distraction. Additionally, some veterans attend college with a brain injury and/or post-traumatic stress. A campus disability office can provide testing and offer various types of accommodations for a range of conditions along with individualized services.

Money

Bursar/Student Accounts
This office processes and collects student tuition, room, and board fees; issues refunds; and collects and disburses financial aid.

Financial Aid
The Financial Aid Office assists students in overcoming financial barriers to their education. The office employs experienced financial advisors who work with students to evaluate their financial needs and obtain federal, state, and/or scholarship assistance to help fund their college education. The Veterans Certifying Official at your college will likely be housed in this office and will serve as the central contact for setting up your VA education benefits.

Student Employment
The Student Employment Center connects students seeking employment with the campus or community entities who are hiring. Here you'll find work study and non-work study jobs posted, as well as volunteer and community service opportunities.

Health & Wellness

Campus Recreation or Athletic Center
Your college probably has at least one athletic center and, if it's a larger school, it might have several, as well as an Outdoor Center, a pool, sports courts and fields, a massage clinic, a climbing gym, and services like fitness evaluations and training and nutrition services.

Counseling Center
Counseling centers provide mental health care, including professional consultation, referral, therapy, academic assessment, emergency services, information and education, and support groups. Similar to a campus disability office, counseling centers are not affiliated with the military or Department of Veterans Affairs in any way and information is not shared between these offices without the written consent of the student. Because of an increase of service members attending college, many campus counselors have received specialized training and are familiar with veterans' diverse needs.

Student Health Services

Many colleges offer students access to some form of quality, affordable and accessible health care services, even if students do not have health insurance. Some colleges have a fully operational hospital, while others have a small clinic. Common services provided by student health centers include immunizations, reduced-cost prescriptions, diagnosis and treatment of common illnesses and minor injuries, pregnancy tests and contraception, and health education outreach.

Campus Life

Campus Police

The goal of the campus police is to create an environment that keeps students safe as they learn, work, live, and play. Your college's campus police may also offer classes on public safety and provide security escorts for students traveling on campus at night.

Center for Spiritual Life/Campus Ministries

The faith center on campus will help connect you to places and people that can support your spiritual life. At many colleges, this center is also actively involved with community outreach and social justice. Whether you're looking for a place to worship, a faith-based study or discussion group, or an opportunity to serve the community, this is a good place to start.

Commuter Student Services

No matter where you live, this office can help you figure out transportation to and from campus. Many Commuter Student Services offices also play a key role in creating and maintaining study areas and other cozy spots that make students feel at home once they're on campus.

Greek Affairs

Sometimes called the Office of Greek Relations, this office supports the educational and social goals of the fraternities and sororities on campus. Resources offered might include academic advising, membership recruitment, leadership development, community service, event planning, risk management, and maintenance of the Greek system facilities.

Multicultural Student Services Center

This office provides information, academic resources, and support for a diverse and inclusive campus community. Many multicultural centers also coordinate diversity training and sponsor campus-wide events related to their mission. Remember, as a veteran, you contribute to making a campus diverse!

Office of Community Service

Community services offices offer volunteer and service-learning opportunities in the greater community.

Ombudsman

An ombudsman is an independent, impartial mediator who assists faculty, staff and students with communication and problem solving. For example, if you believe a faculty member is treating you unfairly and your attempts to resolve the conflict have not been successful, an ombudsman can help you investigate your concerns, meet with relevant parties, and reach a resolution.

Student Union

Most colleges have a student union, which is a dedicated building devoted to student activities. Many unions contain lounges, auditoriums, computer labs, study spaces, and a food court. Some student unions even have bowling alleys, movie theatres, and game rooms! The student union is often described as the "hub" or "heartbeat" of a campus.

Residence Life

Unless they really loved living in the barracks, most veterans opt to live off campus. However, for those who choose to live on campus this office maintains a diverse range of housing and dining options, in addition to facilitating programs and services such as meal plans, room assignments, and roommate matching. Many colleges provide reduced-cost or free room and board in exchange for working as a residence assistant.

Student Activities Center

Student Activities centers plan and organize fun, social, and educational activities both on and off campus for students. Examples include guest speakers, intramural sports leagues, and excursions.

Student Legal Services

Most colleges offer some form of free or reduced-cost legal services. Common cases brought to Student Legal Services staff include tenant-landlord disputes, traffic or alcohol offenses, misdemeanor criminal cases, and consumer complaints. If you are affiliated with the National Guard or Reserves while attending college, this office may be helpful if you are mobilized to active duty and need to break your lease.

Academic Life

Academic Advising

Academic advisors help students plan their schedules, choose their majors, map out a plan for graduation, and set goals for post-graduation. Refer to the Academic Planning chapter, page 36, for an in-depth discussion of this department.

Bookstore

The college bookstore is a hub of academic life, a place to meet up with friends and part with funds. Bookstores offer students all the textbooks and other materials they'll need for their classes. Most bookstores also offer used books at a reduced cost, and end-of-term book buy-back programs.

Computer/Information Technology (IT) Center

Your IT center helps you establish your college email account and network storage. It may also offer computer classes and help with computer-related questions.

Computer Labs

While most students have personal computers, they might use campus computer labs for some projects, to get hands-on assistance with their technology, or for printing jobs. Computer labs are also used as instructional spaces.

Honors Program

Most colleges have an Honors program that offers more challenging academics for advanced or gifted students. Access to this program typically is limited to applicants who meet certain criteria. Those students accepted receive additional support for their rigorous academic schedule. There is also a national honor society for high achieving veterans called SALUTE. **salute.colostate.edu/**

Library

Every college has a central library that students can use to conduct research, find recreational reading materials, or use as a quiet place to study. Most colleges also have departmental libraries. These libraries carry a more extensive selection of materials related to the specific department's needs.

Registrar

The registrar performs a range of student services, including course scheduling, fee waivers, residency and enrollment issues, transcripts, grade reporting and billing.

Tutoring Center/Writing Lab/Math Lab

Tutoring centers and labs are a great resource—and they're often free. They are generally staffed by students with advanced skills who have been trained to tutor others. Some require appointments while others encourage drop-in visits. For individual tutoring services, the VA will provide financial assistance. For more information, go to **www.benefits.va.gov/gibill/tutorial_assistance.asp**

Professional Development

Alumni Association

Alumni associations are established to develop long-term relationships with students. You don't have to be a graduate to benefit from the alumni office. In fact, many of its programs are for current students. Alumni associations promote business networking and career development opportunities, special discount programs and social events. It's also a great way to connect with graduates who are interested in sharing their experience and expertise.

Career Services

Familiarize yourself with this center early on! You'll find internship placements, resumé development assistance, interviewing and networking support, career development classes and publications, job fairs, and job boards. Career services is a go-to office for learning how to articulate your military background into civilian language while getting information on military-friendly employers and career fairs.

Online Resources

You will surely find all of the resources listed above—and others—online. Set aside some time to explore your school's website. Take a virtual tour of the campus and community, sign up for various electronic mailing lists or text notifications, find the central event calendar, and familiarize yourself with the course catalog and department web pages.

Veteran-Specific Resources

Community Organizations

Once you've familiarized yourself with your campus, take some time to familiarize yourself with the greater community. Community-based veterans organizations are excellent resources for meeting other service members, learning about the area, networking, and getting peer to peer support. The links below will assist you with finding a local chapter in your community.

American Legion
www.legion.org/

Veterans of Foreign Wars
www.vfw.org/

Marine Corps League
www.mcleague.org/

Military Officers Association of America
www.moaa.org/

Iraq and Afghanistan Veterans of America
iava.org/

Veterans Office

To accommodate the growing number of veterans in higher education, many colleges have a designated veterans office to serve as a bridge and support student veterans with their transition to campus. The veterans office can offer advocacy in areas related to VA education benefits, federal work study opportunities, housing, academic services, and peer mentoring. It can also provide referrals to other campus-based and community offices. Be sure to contact the veterans office immediately after receiving your acceptance letter.

Student Veterans of America
www.studentveterans.org

Many colleges have a Student Veterans of America chapter that works closely with the veterans office to provide resources and support to student veterans. The SVA is the student veteran voice on campus and their entire mission revolves around advocacy for service members. An SVA chapter is a great way to meet other veterans and learn more about your college from a peer's perspective. Many SVA chapters also spearhead a variety of social and philanthropic activities that support veterans in their communities.

Veterans Upward Bound
www2.ed.gov/programs/triovub/index.html

This free U.S. Department of Education program is designed to motivate veterans and provide refresher training in key subject areas. Many colleges participate in VUB and provide mentoring along with individual instruction with the goal that veterans will complete their postsecondary education program and enter into meaningful career fields.

State Veterans Office
www.va.gov/statedva.htm

Each state maintains a designated office for veterans. Many states also provide county representatives that provide information on benefits, VA home loans, employment services, and disability support. A variety of scholarships and grants for veterans and their dependents may also be available.

Department of Veterans Affairs
www.va.gov

The VA has a multifaceted mission to support veterans in several ways. Navigating the VA can be tricky and overwhelming given the vast number of services provided. Based on this, the veterans office at your college or in your county is an excellent starting point for getting individualized guidance and coming up with a plan. While getting started, refer to the links below for an overview of services and eligibility.

Summary of VA Benefits
benefits.va.gov/BENEFITS/benefits_summary_materials.asp

VA Education Benefits
www.benefits.va.gov/gibill/

VA Healthcare Benefits
www.va.gov/HEALTHBENEFITS/index.asp

Vocational Rehabilitation & Employment
www.benefits.va.gov/vocrehab/

VA Regional Office Finder
benefits.va.gov/benefits/offices.asp

Vet Center Program
www.vetcenter.va.gov

The Vet Center Program provides a range of readjustment counseling services to eligible veterans and their families in an effort to support a successful transition from the military to civilian life. Because many college-based counseling offices only offer a limited number of sessions to their students, a Vet Center is an excellent resource for ongoing services. Another advantage of a Vet Center, aside from being free, is that you will be working with clinicians who are experienced working with military populations. Services provided through Vet Centers include

- individual and group counseling for veterans

- family counseling for military-related issues

- military sexual trauma counseling and referral

- substance abuse assessment and referral

- employment assessment and referral

- screening and referral for medical issues including traumatic brain injury, depression, and post-traumatic stress

1-877-WAR-VETS Call Center
1-877-WAR-VETS is a 24-hour confidential call center where combat veterans and their families can talk about their military experiences or any other issues they are facing in their readjustment to civilian life. The staff is comprised of combat veterans from several eras.

National Resource Directory
https://m.nrd.gov/

The NRD is a comprehensive directory that provides access to thousands of services and resources at the national, state and local levels to support recovery, rehabilitation and reintegration. Service members, veterans, family members and caregivers can find information on key topics such as health care, employment, education, and counseling. Their handy search engine allows you to locate resources by state and zip code.

Military One Source
www.militaryonesource.mil/

Military One Source is a confidential Department of Defense-funded program that provides thorough information on many aspects of military life at no cost to active duty, National Guard and Reserve members, and their families. Key information categories include, but are not limited to, deployment, relationship, mental health, employment and education, and parenting and childhood services.

Campus Activities

CHAPTER 3

As a veteran you know how to think strategically and with an end goal in mind. Therefore, you might be inclined to approach college classes with great intensity. However, a better strategy is to pace yourself and learn how to invest your time and energy wisely. A schedule that only includes going to class and putting in long hours at the library will quickly lead to burnout. And let's be real here – a lifestyle like that is just not fun. Your time on campus offers you many ways to be active and campus activities play a vital part in making you a well-rounded and successful student.

Consider This ...

Why Get Involved?

- Meet new people
- Make connections
- Play
- Develop skills
- Stay in shape
- Build your resumé

The variety of organizations, sports groups, and other social clubs available to you is endless and appeals to every interest imaginable, from niche groups (Mixed Martial Arts) to broad, nationally-based organizations (Amnesty International). Having served in the military, you're no stranger to taking risks and seeking out adventure. Apply that same curiosity and willingness to push yourself past your comfort zone in this new environment; after all, there's no better time than now to try new things.

This chapter will discuss the following:

- The bigger picture: Why extracurricular activities are truly important
- Types of campus activities
- How to choose activities to participate in
- How and why to commit to your chosen activities

The Bigger Picture

You may wonder why something non-academic is so important. Common sense suggests that you go to college to attend classes and study, right? Although these are crucial parts of being a successful student, participating in activities can hone your career and life skills.

For example, the ability to communicate effectively and give engaging presentations is a vital skill set that employers rank as one of the most desirable qualities of a newly hired employee. By participating in a debate club or holding a leadership position in a student organization, you are already showing initiative and the capacity to take charge. Another point to consider is that research shows that students that participate in extracurricular activities feel more connected to their college and are subsequently more likely to remain enrolled through graduation.

Types of Campus Activities

There are as many on-campus activities as there are student interests. Some are one-time or seasonal events that anybody can participate in. Check out the event calendar at your college as well as your academic department to find out what is going on around campus. You'll find plays, poetry readings, film screenings, multicultural events, debates, and outings that are open to anyone.

Here's an overview to get you thinking of places where you might want to get involved:

Culture and Identity

Some groups are formed based on the culture or identity of their members. Latino student associations, LGBTQ, and Student Veterans of America are examples.

> The most challenging part of my transition out of the Army has been finding people I can connect with. Getting involved with a student organization and finding people who share similar interests is a smart thing to do.
>
> **Justin, Army Veteran**

Religious and Spiritual

Your school might have a specific religious denomination or it might have diverse religious and spiritual affiliations represented.

Greek System

Fraternities and sororities vary in their role, size, mission, and traditions from college to college and from group to group. You can find out more about your school's Greek system—its role on campus, how to join, and expectations for members—through the Greek Affairs Office.

Media

Does your college have a student-run newspaper, radio station, television network, online or print magazine? Depending on the medium and mission, you might find a place on staff as a writer, editor, advertising salesperson, graphic designer, videographer, DJ, etc.

Political

College has long been synonymous with political exploration and activism. From Amnesty International and Greenpeace to College Republicans and College Democrats, you will find a host of political organizations represented on campus.

Consider This ...

When I arrived on campus I was overwhelmed by its size and the fact that I hadn't been a student for several years. Getting connected to our Student Veterans Organization was the best thing for me. I met other veterans; students who were older and who had been through similar experiences in the military that I could relate to. They also weren't in school just to party. The SVO became a close group for me and we spearheaded several fundraising activities that supported veterans in our community in addition to forming study groups and hosting various social events. My advice to a new student veteran is to get involved with a student organization.

Elizabeth, U.S. Navy

Special Interest Groups

These groups are based on the common interests of their members. Photography clubs, distance running, triathlons, and martial arts are a few examples.

Sports

From intercollegiate sports to intramural sports to on-campus teams, leagues, and tournaments, there will be no shortage of ways for you to sweat; throw, hit, and bounce things; yell, shout and laugh; wear funny equipment; and wear yourself out. Lacrosse, skiing, skydiving, basketball, archery, and even bowling appear on lists of sports activities.

Student Government

Nearly every college has a student government. You can participate as an elected officer or representative from your department, residence hall, or club.

Is something missing? Perhaps you want to run one of the hardcore mud obstacle courses that are offered throughout the country or jump out of a perfectly good airplane. If you have an idea for an activity or club, it may be up to YOU to get it started.

How to Choose?

We recommend that you check out a lot of activities now and get a feel for them. Try out those clubs that revolve around things you're already passionate about, but also try out the clubs that spark your curiosity or seem out of your comfort zone. Be open to finding a new passion.

After you've explored your options, reflect on what you hope to gain from your extracurricular activities. Ask yourself:

What is my motivation? Is it to make friends, develop a new skill, relax, help others, and/or get outside?

Which activities fit my needs? Make sure you fully understand the mission, values, and requirements of the organization.

Can I fulfill the requirements of the organization? Some clubs charge dues or initiation fees, or require members to travel and/or purchase uniforms and equipment. Some organizations take attendance and require members to fulfill a certain number of hours per month. Some require members to complete a task or demonstrate a certain skill level—world language clubs may require potential members to pass an oral fluency exam, for example, and scuba diving clubs probably require their members be licensed.

Commit

When you find a group you're interested in, stay in touch and informed via social media. Most campus organizations will have an events calendar you can subscribe to or a Facebook group you can join. If you want to take your commitment to the next level, choose a group or two that you can dedicate your time to. Commitment means attending the meetings and events regularly, showing up on time for activities, being an active participant in meetings and projects, and providing leadership by volunteering for roles within the organization.

Active, meaningful participation will challenge and fulfill you. Sure, you don't want to overextend yourself and spend so much time on activities that your academic work suffers. On the other hand, taking some time to pursue your passions outside the classroom can invigorate and enrich your college experience and lead to promising opportunities down the road.

Campus Activities **Exercises**

1. Make a list of three or four extracurricular activities that interest you. What would be the benefits of getting involved in each activity? What would be the commitment level? What drawbacks, if any, would there be to getting involved in each one?

2. Choose two extracurricular events or activities to participate in this week. Afterwards, take a few minutes to reflect about what you did and what you got out of each experience.

3. Which extracurricular events or activities would give you the chance to be with a diverse group of people? Select one to participate in and write about the experience (or make a presentation about your experience).

Visit **www.LifeDuringCollege.com**
for more resources and exercises.

Campus Safety

CHAPTER 4

As a veteran, you are familiar with tactical thinking, situational awareness, and safeguarding information so that you don't violate OPSEC. If you served overseas, you learned to watch your surroundings carefully and, over time, to spot things out of the ordinary. Although college includes exciting lectures and rich social experiences, it also contains some dangers that require your attention.

Your school's role in keeping you safe is to provide campus police, well-lit walkways, education on potential risks and prevention, emergency training and drills, and to coordinate with state and local agencies to stay abreast of best practices in campus security. Your role is to use these resources and education to guide your behavior.

This chapter will provide an overview of campus safety issues, including

- drinking and drugs
- sexual assault
- burglary and robbery
- identity theft
- stalking and harrassment
- cyber safety
- general safety tips

Drinking and Drugs

Your health and safety are directly affected by your use (or non-use) of alcohol and drugs. The lower your inhibitions and more clouded your judgment the more likely you are to put yourself at risk or to put others at risk. We don't intend to be preachy in this chapter, but we must be real: the college years, especially the early college years, are a time when many people experiment with alcohol and drugs. Binge drinking, while not an exclusively college behavior, is very closely associated with the college experience.

Despite being pervasive on many college campuses, alcohol and drugs are devastating to the health and safety of college students. Much of campus crime and injury is attributable to the use and abuse of alcohol and drugs, as they negatively impact behaviors and impair judgment.

Here are some statistics from the National Institute of Alcohol Abuse and Alcoholism (NIAAA) to remind you of the role these substances play in the lives of college students between the ages of 18 and 24:

- Every year nearly 600,000 students are unintentionally injured while under the influence of alcohol
- More than 97,000 students are victims of alcohol-related sexual assault or acquaintance rape
- 400,000 students had unprotected sex and more than 100,000 report being too intoxicated to know if they consented to having sex
- 1,800 students die each year from alcohol-related injuries, including car crashes

The best thing you can do to protect yourself and others is to stay sober or drink responsibly. If you are in a situation where you feel people have gotten out of control, leave. If you believe others may be at risk, contact the proper authorities. You could save someone's life.

Alcohol Poisoning Symptoms

Seek help if you notice someone exhibiting the following symptoms:

- **confusion, stupor**
- **vomiting**
- **seizures**
- **slow or irregular breathing**
- **blue-ish or pale skin**
- **low body temperature**
- **unconsciousness**

GOOD To KNOW

Note: Alcohol poisoning does not necessarily involve all of these symptoms.

Source: The Mayo Clinic (www.mayoclinic.com)

Sexual Assault

We'll focus on facts and tips related to the most common type of sexual assault (a female victim and a male perpetrator), though males of course can be victims of sexual attacks. Sexual assault of all forms is widely believed to be underreported. According to a recent US Department of Justice report on sexual assault of college campuses,

- nearly 5% of college women are assaulted in a given year
- 90% of college women who are raped know their attacker
- most women are more concerned about "stranger danger" than the possibility of being attacked by an acquaintance, friend, ex-boyfriend, or other known person

TIP Most colleges have a dedicated center that offers support and training on sexual assault awareness and prevention.

Campus security escorts and defense training are available at most colleges. By all means take advantage of these resources—just remember the safest bet is to stick with a group of trusted friends. Friends should watch out for each other, especially at parties, to make sure no one is left isolated and vulnerable to a bad situation or that no one gets out of control and acts in a threatening manner toward someone else.

TIP

DO NOT accept drinks from people, or leave your cup sitting around at a party. I've seen so many people roofied!

Jamie H., Sophomore, Olympia, WA

Be particularly careful around alcohol, as it is considered the #1 date-rape drug because it lowers inhibitions. To make matters worse, some perpetrators will slip sedatives, such as Rohypnol ("Roofie"), into drinks of unsuspecting partygoers. Such drugs have an amnesiac effect, and leave victims vulnerable to attack.

Burglary and Robbery

By far the most common on-campus crime is burglary. While you don't need a special pickpocket-proof wallet or a wrist cuff for your laptop, take reasonable precautions to protect your valuables in your apartment and when you're out and about on campus. Also, if you have a bike, invest in a good bike lock and use it.

When you're off campus, try not to carry valuables or a lot of cash. Avoid ATMs in isolated or sketchy areas.

Most common criminal offenses on US campuses (in order):

Consider This ...

1. Burglary
2. Motor vehicle theft
3. Aggravated assault
4. Sex offenses—forcible
5. Robbery
6. Arson

Source: US Dept. of Postsecondary Education

Identity Theft

Who are you? You might delve into the depths of this question in Philosophy or Identity Politics. But in this section we're mostly just talking about your name, your social security number, and your cash.

Identity theft is when someone steals your name and personal information for their financial gain. It can come in many forms and the effects can be devastating financially for several years. College students are particularly vulnerable to identity theft because they receive frequent credit card applications, tend to store personal information on their computers and cell phones, and infrequently reconcile their bank or credit card balances. Even if you don't have many assets right now (a microwave, ten pairs of socks, and a stack of textbooks), thieves can steal your future earnings by racking up debt in your name now.

GooD To KNow

Prevent identify theft on campus by

- shredding credit card applications and other documents that might contain personal information
- using a firewall on your computer
- carefully reviewing bank documents and financial aid documents
- Keeping your PINs and passwords to yourself

Stalking and Harrassment

Harassment and stalking are other problems that college-aged students encounter more frequently than other age groups. According to the United

States Department of Justice, there are "seven types of harassing or unwanted behaviors consistent with stalking":

- making unwanted phone calls;

- sending unsolicited or unwanted letters or emails;

- following or spying on the victim;

- showing up at a place where they had no reason to be;

- waiting at places for the victim;

- leaving unwanted items, presents, or flowers;

- posting information or spreading rumors about the victim on the Internet, in a public place, or by word of mouth.

If you have experienced two or more of these behaviors on two or more separate occasions and if you fear for your safety, notify campus police.

Cyber Safety

Here are some things you can do right now to ensure your cyber safety:

Protect yourself by using privacy settings, lock screens, and preventative software. Make sure that if you lose your phone or lose track of your tablet no one would be able to access the personal information it contains. You can install anti-theft software that allows you to lock your device remotely. You can also install anti-virus software to protect yourself from malware. The cost of the protective software will be well worth it if your computer, tablet, or phone is compromised.

About Cyber Safety

Consider This ...

Have images of you or other personal information been posted online without your consent? Go to withoutmyconsent.org to see what you can do.

www.withoutmyconsent.org

Password protect your laptop, other devices, and accounts. Make sure you don't share your password and make sure the password is strong. Don't trust your memory to retain anything but your pet's name and birthdate? Consider using an app like PasswordBox or LastPass to organize and protect your various passwords.

Recognize phishing. "Phishing" is an email fraud scam. If you receive an email that seems legitimate—say, from your bank or your school—and it asks you to verify an important piece of personal information, such as your social security number, do not click. Do not verify information, even if it's just your email address, until you call the supposed source of the request and verify that it is indeed legitimate.

Avoid using public computers or WiFi for private communication or shopping. Public computers may have a keystroke logger that records everything you type. Insecure networks might expose you to malicious mischief or worse.

Remember that nothing's temporary online. Post and share only that information and those images that you'd feel comfortable sharing with a wide audience—

because it's always possible that you'll have a wider audience than you intended. Your activity on Snapchat, WhatsApp, and Facebook is a few clicks away from being shared with the world.

Don't be a cyber criminal. Let's say you're broke. Let's say you want some new music or a free movie. File sharing software and peer-to-peer (P2P) services make it easy to share music and movies. However, if doing so violates copyright then it would be stealing. It's a common crime, but a crime nonetheless. Check out respectcopyrights.org for more information, including this reminder that they have posted: "You are not anonymous."

Other Tips and Information

Colleges are required to file crime statistics with the federal government. Go to **http://ope.ed.gov/security/** if you're curious for more information about your school.

Check around your campus and community for safety education and workshops. Attending an orientation or class will help you learn more about the resources and considerations particular to your school and its environs.

We'll end this chapter with these good general tips:

Be aware of your surroundings and the people around you. Pay attention to where your belongings are at all times.

Familiarize yourself with your campus—know where well-lighted paths, emergency phones, and campus police stations are located.

Keep your cell phone on you and store emergency numbers so you can dial them easily.

Try to avoid being alone in isolated areas of the campus, such as the basement laundry room or even your own apartment when other students are not close by.

Protect your privacy. Don't list your picture, name, and contact information where people can easily access it. Assume that information you post on social networking sites is available to the general public.

If you notice another person in danger, call 911 or campus security. Do not engage with another person who has a weapon.

Do not use ATMs after dark or in isolated places.

Don't carry a lot of cash or valuables. Cash, nice jewelry, and other valuables are easy targets for thieves.

Do not accept drinks from others, as drinks can easily be drugged.

GOOD TO KNOW

National Crisis Hotlines

Important numbers to know if you or a friend needs information or help:

National AIDS Hotline
1-800-CDC-INFO (1-800-232-4636) (Center for Disease Control)

Alcohol and Drug Abuse
1-800-729-6686 (Substance Abuse and Mental Health Services Administration)

Cutting and Self-Abuse
1-800-DONT-CUT (1-800-366-8288) (Self Abuse Finally Ends organization)

Eating Disorders
1-800-931-2237 (National Eating Disorder Organization)

Pregnancy
1-800-230-PLAN (1-800-230-7526) (Planned Parenthood Hotline)

Rape, Sexual Abuse, and Incest
1-800-656-HOPE (1-800-656-4673) (RAINN Rape Crisis Hotline)

Suicide Hotline
1-800-273-TALK (1-800-273-8255)

Academic Planning
A Different Type of Land Nav

CHAPTER 5

In college, you should customize your academic plan to best suit your individual interests. When you joined the military you selected a Military Occupational Specialty (MOS); most likely, you did so after researching your options, taking the ASVAB, and speaking with your recruiter about all of the different career fields available. Similarly, crafting your academic plan requires a good bit of self-reflection as well as forecasting what you see yourself doing in the future. In other words, it is a process of exploration that involves asking questions, setting goals and taking action while constantly assessing your progress along the way.

To get started, consider the following questions: What kind of job would I enjoy going to each day? What types of subjects hold my interest? Is my area of interest best suited as a hobby or a career? How can I match my education to my long-term goals?

This chapter will discuss the following:

- Your academic advisor and you

- Selecting a major and minor

- Changing your major

- Developing a graduation plan

- Selecting and registering for classes

Your Academic Advisor

Your academic advisor is an invaluable resource to keep you on course when you're navigating the college landscape. Ideally, your academic advisor is an approachable, caring, knowledgeable mentor who will inform you about options and requirements and help guide you in your decision making. Usually, your advisor is assigned to you. He or she might be a full-time professional advisor or a professor in your chosen field of study who also advises students. At this early stage your "chosen field" is whatever box you checked when you sent in your initial paperwork. You have the option to change advisors.

If you decide to switch, take time to find the advisor who best meets your needs. Talk to students and professors to get recommendations. Speaking with other veterans on campus or identifying an advisor who is experienced working with non-traditional students are excellent starting points for finding a good match. You may also want to meet with several different advisors to discuss your situation and your goals.

Bring a copy of your DD214 and military transcript when you meet with your advisor. Many veterans have completed military training and have experiences that can result in the awarding of college credit. Bring your military transcript along with any completed CLEP or DANTES courses to your meeting with your advisor. You can also direct your advisor to the American Council on Education (ACE) Military Evaluation webpage to determine if your service background qualifies for awarding equivalent college credit: **http://www.acenet. edu/higher-education/topics/Pages/Military-Evaluations.aspx**

Selecting a Major / Minor

Most colleges require students to declare a major in the latter part of their sophomore year or the beginning of their junior year. Check with your student handbook or your academic advisor for your college's requirements.

Selecting a major may be a carefully weighed decision, it may be a leap of faith, or it may be a little of both. You will find a variety of advice when it comes to deciding on your path to graduation and beyond. Some say "follow your bliss." Others say "follow the money." Only you can decide what is best for you.

Take tests. Visit your Counseling Center or Career Center and see what types of aptitude and personality tests are offered. Identify your strengths and interests.

Make a list. Write a list of the topics, classes and careers that interest you.

Do research and ask questions. What types of majors and minors stand out for the careers you're interested in? What percentage of graduates actually end up working in a field related to their major? What is an average starting salary for a specific major?

Talk to the experts. Talk to people who work in a field you find interesting. Check out your college's Career Center or Alumni Office – the staff can put you in contact with all sorts of resources, including alumni who have volunteered to mentor students.

Get hands on. Nothing beats hands-on experience for finding out what you like. Check with the Career Center and speak with other veterans about work-study and volunteer opportunities and internships.

Map out the educational commitment. Many careers require additional education beyond the initial college diploma. You may have several years of classes ahead of you, along with residencies, apprenticeships, and so on. Because many veterans qualify for a combination of federal and state benefits, be sure to consult with the Veterans Office to maximize your financial awards.

Meet with the Veterans Certifying Official. If you intend to use VA education benefits, be sure that your academic program and classes are approved by the VCO. Also be sure to contact the VCO if you change your major or withdraw.

Consider the Career

Where can you go and what can you do with your major? While you may love the content of business management classes, if the thought of leading, advising, and managing people terrifies you then Business Management is not the major for you. When selecting a major, carefully consider what kinds of career options it would lead to. Also, be sure to think about technology and how it can impact a career. Some majors and occupations are quickly becoming obsolete, while others are up and coming and are forecasted to grow.

Evaluate your personality. How does your personality suit your major's career options? Are you a people person or do you prefer working with numbers and facts? Are you a team player or someone who works better alone? Do you thrive on change or crave routine?

Map out the educational commitment. Many careers require more education after the initial college diploma. You may have two, four, six, even seven more years of classes, residencies, apprenticeships, and so on.

> *The greatest obstacle to discovery is not ignorance—it is the illusion of knowledge.*
> **Daniel J. Boorstin, American Historian**

Consider career conditions. What kinds of hours do you want to work? Would you thrive in a profession that has busy and slow seasons? Do you like to work on tight deadlines and in a fast-paced environment? Do you like autonomy or would you feel comfortable working within an organizational structure?

Evaluate earning power. Some professions have higher earning potential than others. How important is money to you and your future? What kind of lifestyle would you like to have and what kinds of commitments and sacrifices are you willing to make for it? The U.S. Department of Labor has all sorts of interesting information about careers on its website, including how much various professions make, and what the projected need is for workers in those professions: http://www.bls.gov/

Hot Jobs! Here are some of the fastest growing professions, according to the Bureau of Labor Statistics:

Consider This ...

- interpreters/translators
- genetic counselors
- physician assistants
- information security analysts
- health specialties teachers
- physical therapists
- nurse practitioners
- meeting, convention and event planners

Changing Your Major

Many students begin working on one major and then switch after they discover something new and exciting about another major or after they realize that their current one isn't the right fit. You can change your major. In fact, the average college student will change his or her major at least twice. The more frequently you change majors and the later on in the process you make the change, the more costly it gets. You might graduate later than you planned or pay for classes that were unnecessary to your degree. However, switching majors in college is less costly than completing one degree and then coming back to school years later to earn the degree you really want.

> *I'd rather fail at doing something I love than succeed at doing something I hate.*
> **George Burns, American humorist**

Selecting a Minor or a Double Major

Selecting two majors or a minor is a good way to get the most out of your college experience. Of course it can be difficult and time-consuming, too. Before committing to a double major or a minor, consider the following:

Decide as early as possible so you can develop a good course schedule and graduate in a timely manner.

Limit your electives. Because of the number of classes required to fulfill a double major or a major/minor, your schedule will not have room for many electives.

Select thoughtfully. Do your majors complement each other? Will the combination add to your range and career choices? Is it reasonable to pursue the two majors in four or five years?

Think of your academic plan as a work in progress: in the first year it's very malleable. With flexibility and foresight—and some help from your academic advisor and others—you can customize an academic plan that has room for experimentation *and* graduation.

Developing a Graduation Plan

We know people on the "four-year plan" or the "five-year plan" and even some on the "ten-year plan." The "plan" in this case refers to a person's graduation plan. Some students decide their major, then schedule exactly those courses they need to graduate in exactly four years. They know their destination and they take the Interstate to get there: It's direct and fast. Others take a bit longer to decide on a major or they choose to pursue additional degrees (another major, perhaps? A minor? Two?). This is like travelling with a general idea of your destination and taking a combination of major highways and scenic byways to get there. A few students truly meander or are diverted by time, interest, or money and graduate later than their cohort group. The time it takes you to graduate is up to you and your interests and circumstances. No one gets a medal for coming in first. On the other hand, it can get pretty expensive to take classes that don't relate to your major or minor. It's handy to have a map, even if you don't end up following it precisely the way you intended to. Here's how to develop a graduation plan:

Use the course catalog. Most college course catalogs provide sample graduation schedules. You can create your individualized plan based on these examples.

Pay attention to prerequisites. Upper level classes usually have prerequisites, classes you are required to take before you move on. Make sure you fulfill the prerequisites early on so you'll be able to fit in all the courses required for your major.

Check in with your advisor. Your academic advisor knows the big picture and the little details, as well as insider information like which classes are really exciting but have a dull title.

Sample some classes. If you are unsure about the major you want to pursue, take introductory courses that will give you a sampling of the majors you are considering. This way you'll broaden your experience and find the major that really sparks your passion. Another way to explore your options is to audit a course or sit in on a couple of class sessions.

Don't miss out. Some classes are offered on a rotating basis: first level first term, second level second term. Others are offered sporadically. Sometimes there's an incredible professor who teaches a course once every other year or so. Find out about these special offerings—check with your advisor or ask other students—and plan accordingly.

Achieve balance. Easier said than done, we know! Balance in this context means registering for a combination of difficult and easier courses each term to avoid unnecessary stress. It also means regulating your credit load: Refer to your college's recommendations for the number of credits per term. You don't want to overload and burn out or perform poorly in that term; you also don't want to take so few credits that you lose momentum or lose out on financial aid.

Consider summer school, online classes, etc.

You now have the option to take classes anytime and anywhere. Taking a couple of classes during the summer will give you more flexibility during the school year. (Also, the more credits you have, the higher priority you'll have for registration.)

Graduation Planning Calculator

Adventures in Education, a service of the Texas Guaranteed Student Loan Corporation, has a great online calculator that students can use to budget their time in college—as well as their finances. **www.aie.org**

Selecting Classes

Ah, the course catalog! So many possibilities! How should you choose which classes to take?

Find out what's required. Most colleges have undergraduate minimum requirements that all students must fulfill. You will also have required courses in your department once you've declared a major. Check and double check the course catalog to make sure you're taking the right classes at the right level. (For example, a university requirement might be to take at least ten credit hours in math and the 200 level and above. If that's the case, Math 121 won't fulfill that requirement.) Your academic advisor will help you evaluate your high school transcript and college entrance exams to determine what course levels you should begin with.

Research the course. Start by reading the full description in the catalog. If you need more details, contact the department or instructor or go to the relevant website. Talk to your advisor and to other students who have taken the course. You may find reviews online or in a campus publication—these can be helpful, but they can be misleading, too. Course reviews are by nature subjective.

What another student calls "impossible and confusing" you might call "challenging and intriguing." Is the instructor good? Is the class easy? For some students these are the same questions, for others they're quite distinct.

Research the instructor. Word gets around: This instructor is incredible! That professor's lectures are amazing! You'll hear about instructors who inspire and provoke, who challenge students and change lives. Their teaching style might be traditional or avant garde, their classes might be lecture-based or experiential, but there's something about them that makes an impression on students. Try to sign up for such classes when you have a chance even if they don't fulfill a requirement—the worst thing that could happen is you take an awesome class from a great teacher, the best thing that could happen is you discover a passion for a subject you didn't know about before. If you hear through the grapevine about an instructor who is ineffective, follow up on that information with more research. There are some classes that you might want to avoid. You only have so much time and money and you want to make the most of your education.

Challenge a course when appropriate. If for some reason you are not satisfied with the course level you were assigned, you may want to challenge a course. This usually involves taking a placement exam that covers the material that would normally have been presented in the course. If you pass the exam, you are not required to take the course and can move on to higher level classes. Most colleges levy a fee for the process of challenging a course—and a student will have to pay the fee whether or not their challenge is successful. Also, if you do pass the exam you may have to pay for being awarded credits for the course.

Again, check with your advisor before beginning the process.

Registering for Classes

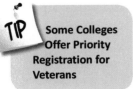
TIP

Some Colleges
Offer Priority
Registration for
Veterans

The process of registering for classes varies from campus to campus but you can count on some element of surprise and anxiety until you are a junior or senior and you get top pick of classes. Classes can get filled or canceled. Based on this, build your ideal schedule in advance, knowing that you'll need to be flexible on the day of registration. Another tip to consider is that many colleges offer priority registration to veterans. Be sure to check with your advisor and the Veteran's Office to maximize your registration and always come prepared with a backup plan just in case. Here are other things to keep in mind as you create your schedule:

Your commitments. Do you have a work schedule? Family commitments? Extracurricular activities? Make sure you plan your classes accordingly. If you will be working until midnight most nights you probably don't want to schedule an 8:00 a.m. class. If you have a major sports tournament coming up, you may want to limit the number of challenging classes you take that term.

Your biological clock. The one that tells you to wake up at 5:00 a.m. and feel drowsy at 3:00 p.m. (or vice versa). By now you know when you're most alert, most able to learn, and most energized. Schedule classes and homework time for those hours, if possible. It's easy to find energy to play Ultimate Frisbee or to chat with a friend, but it's difficult to muster energy to sit through hundreds of slides of ancient artifacts—if those hundreds of slides are projected onto a screen in a dark, warm room when you're at your sleepiest.

What's Your Prime Time?

When am I most alert?

When am I sleepiest?

What's my most productive time of the day?

When am I least focused?

Visit **www.LifeDuringCollege.com**
for more resources and exercises.

Your downtime. You need to get from one class to the next. You need to eat. You need to study. (OK, maybe studying doesn't count as downtime. But "non-class time" has a certain awkwardness to it, so we'll file it in this category.) Be deliberate about your class schedule *and* your break schedule.

> **TIP**
> Have alternative course times available when registering for your classes in case your first choices are not available.

Do everything in your power to create an ideal schedule, make sure your bills and fines are paid up (sometimes the most miniscule fine can keep you from registering!), preview the registration process, get instructor approval for those classes that require it, have your pins and passwords handy, and register the very moment it's open to you.

The Filled Class

You researched and planned. You tapped in the right numbers at the right time and…you were denied. The filled class is one of the frustrations of the first year of college. One remedy is to take a breath and see what else is available. If you really have your heart set on that class, you can contact the instructor directly and ask if he or she would be willing and able to make an exception. Or you can ask the instructor if she or he will allow you to attend the class through the add/drop period and take the spot of a registered student who decides to drop the course. You may even be able to register for an open section of the course, but attend the lectures of the closed class. Make sure your instructor is on board with this switch and confirm that the lectures and content for the two classes are identical before you attempt this creative approach.

Academic Planning **Exercises**

1. Review all the majors your school offers and research at least two that interest you. What are the credit requirements for each major? What kinds of prerequisites are there for each major? Which classes in the subject seem particularly interesting? Which classes in the subject seem particularly difficult or not interesting? What kinds of internships or apprenticeships are related to each major? What kinds of career opportunities are there?

2. Which resources were most helpful in answering the questions above?

3. Take an aptitude or personality test at your college career center or counseling office. Or, if those tests are unavailable on campus, take one online. Reflect on your results: According to the test, what are your strengths, weaknesses, personality traits, and interests? Which education or career paths do the results suggest for you? What did you learn about yourself (or about the test) through this process?

4. Outline your ideal week: When would you attend classes? When would you study? What extracurricular activities would you do and when? When would you sleep and eat? How much time would you spend socializing and what kinds of socializing would you prefer? What other things would you do with your time?

5. What resources are available to find out more about a class or instructor at your college?

Visit **www.LifeDuringCollege.com**
for more resources and exercises.

Strategic Relationships & Allies

CHAPTER 6

College is a prime time for meeting people and making connections. As you experienced in the military, you are surrounded by people from a variety of backgrounds and interests. You have instructors from all over the world, instructors with experience and research in fascinating and sometimes obscure fields. The student body and faculty are diverse, but everybody has one thing in common. Your fellow students and you have chosen to attend this college and your instructors have chosen to teach at this college. You share a campus, a town, and at least some values – you believe in the importance of education, for example. This kernel of shared interest is what makes college an experience instead of simply a series of classes one takes.

Your relationships with instructors and other students will in many ways define your college experience. This chapter covers the following topics:

- Developing relationships with your instructors
- Getting to know your instructor outside the classroom
- Emailing and meeting with your instructors
- Difficulties with instructors
- Developing relationships with your classmates

Developing Relationships with Your Instructors

In the military you learned the chain of command, a hierarchical system that ascribes certain privileges, expectations, and status depending on a person's rank. Generally, a seasoned rank (e.g. Sergeant Major or Colonel) meant a more knowledgeable leader with vast experience in a given field. In college there is also a chain of command among instructors that ranges from teaching assistants, adjuncts, and lecturers and progresses all the way through assistant, associate, and full professors. Some may have extensive experience in their field and in teaching, while others may just be starting their academic careers. Some encourage formality and others prefer an informal teaching style. Ideally, all your instructors will have a passion for teaching.

Inevitably you will have instructors who don't teach according to your learning style. Also, you will find yourself in a variety of classroom environments. You might be in a class of 8 students or in a lecture hall with 500 students. Keep an open mind—you might think you need hands-on experiential learning, but find that a passionate lecturer is your favorite professor. You might feel lost in a cavernous lecture hall until you make a connection with the teaching assistant assigned to your section and realize that she or he's a great teacher. Developing a relationship with your instructor depends on him or her, the situation (the number of other students, the setting, the class time and place, etc.), and you. Here's what you can do to make positive connections with your instructors in class:

Attend class regularly and on time. Research has shown that attendance is the most important factor in student success in a course. In fact, one study calculated the cost of each missed class session to be .06 points off a student's G.P.A. Aside from academic performance, another way to look at class attendance is with regard to your investment in your education. For example, your instructor may be an expert in his or her field who charges an expensive hourly fee for consulting services. Missing a class is therefore missing out on invaluable information that you're already paying for. If you know you will miss a class, contact your instructor and inform him or her of the situation, then make sure to take action to acquire notes or other missed material.

Sit near the front of the class, where your instructor will notice you and where you'll be more likely to stay engaged in the lecture or discussion.

Complete the reading, homework, and the suggested but optional readings before class. Try to have at least one or two core speaking points that you can share.

Participate in class discussions. An interesting class depends on interested students. Do your part to add to class discussion.

Ask questions. Pursue your curiosity and interest. Also, ask questions of other students to facilitate a dynamic class discussion.

Avoid asking certain questions, such as "Is this going to be on the exam?" and "Did I miss anything?" In general, instructors want to engage students in learning, not simply to inform students how to perform for a grade. Assume you did miss something if you missed class.

Demonstrate open-mindedness and respect for your instructor. This includes addressing him or her by the proper title and pronouncing his or her name correctly. Let your instructor set the tone on formality.

Avoid disruptions and negative attention. Turn off or silence your phone before entering class. Make sure your actions and body language convey interest in class. Slumping, texting, and madly scribbling in one's daily planner all communicate "I'd rather be somewhere else, anywhere else, with someone else!" even if what you're actually texting is "This class is amazing!" Also, if you know you'll have to leave class early, let your instructor know at the beginning of class. Finally, eat or drink in class only if you know it is acceptable with your instructor.

Disclosing your Military Service

Some students choose to withhold their veteran status while others are comfortable sharing their military history with their instructors. Because of your unique experiences and ability to enhance course material, your instructors may call on you to discuss your military background with the class. If this is something that you are uncomfortable doing, be sure to inform your instructors to avoid a potentially uncomfortable situation.

Getting to Know Your Instructor Outside of the Classroom

Outside of the classroom, you can create other opportunities to develop a relationship with your instructor. Take time to visit with your instructors—take advantage of their offers to assist students, and ask for help and advice when you need it. Generally instructors enjoy this aspect of their job very much. Also, try to attend any out-of-class gatherings or field trips where you'll be able to learn more about the subject you're studying and connect with instructors and classmates.

Here are some reasons you might meet with your instructor outside of class:

- To request guidance on a paper topic, research project, or other issue
- To ask him or her to point you to resources to help you succeed in class
- To learn more about your instructor's area of expertise or her or his department
- To obtain advice about how to do better on future assignments and exams
- To make contacts within an industry in order to get an internship or job
- To seek guidance on future education and career plans

Bigger Picture — Letters of Recommendation

If you do end up developing a strong relationship with your instructor, you may ask him or her to act as your mentor or your academic advisor. A favorable relationship with your instructor may open all sorts of doors for teaching, research, or an internship in addition to strengthening your knowledge of a given field. Also, scholarships, employers, and graduate schools almost always require letters of recommendation from applicants. Based on these points, you will want at least a couple of instructors who know you well and who will be willing to write you an academic letter of recommendation.

Emailing Your Instructors

Always, always, treat an email to an instructor with the same care you would an old-fashioned letter. That is, include an appropriate salutation (*Dear Dr. So-and-So,*), proper spelling, capitalization, and punctuation, and a closing statement. While there may be some exceptions, most of the instructors we know and work with grimace at sloppy, informal emails. Also, make sure the content of your email is something you'd feel comfortable talking about in person. If you have a question about why you received a certain grade on a test, for example, use the email only to request an appointment to discuss your concern.

Use email...

To request an appointment. Include the purpose for the appointment and propose a time or two that might work: "Would you be able to meet with me on Wednesday afternoon to discuss possible paper topics?"

To request clarification on an assignment if there is no opportunity to do so face-to-face. Before you use email for this purpose, make sure you have thoroughly read the directions provided.

To inform your instructor about something. For example, you might email to say you won't be in class for a couple of days because you are ill. No need to go into detail—just give information that is relevant to him or her.

As suggested by the instructor. Some instructors prefer email communication and invite their students to discuss topics with them via email.

To confirm information or an agreement. Example: "Thank you for meeting with me today. I appreciate your granting me an extension until next Tuesday."

Never use email...

If you need an immediate response. Assume you won't get a response to an email for 24 hours.

To ask about why you got a certain grade. Email is too cumbersome for this purpose and you'll miss a good opportunity to improve as a student. Request an appointment, then bring in the paper or test so you can discuss it in person. She or he can elaborate on written comments and you might ask for ways you might improve in the future.

To complain or confront. If you feel strongly about a grade or issue, you should request an appointment and talk privately with your instructor. Face-to-face communication is much more effective for these situations: you will be more likely to come to a mutual understanding if you approach your instructor personally and with an open mind.

To include your instructor in your circle of friends. Refrain from forwarding mass emails or sending very personal messages to your instructors.

Meeting with Your Instructors

With a few exceptions, your instructors will be very busy people who try to make themselves available to students as much as possible.

Here are some tips for planning to meet with your instructors:

Schedule an appointment. Even if your instructor holds regular office hours, try to schedule an appointment to ensure you get to meet with him or her during that time.

Earlier is better. Like you, your instructor will have more competing issues to deal with as her or his day progresses. To get your instructor's full attention, schedule your meetings as early in her or his daily schedule as possible.

Be on time. Locate your instructor's office prior to your scheduled appointment and make sure you get there when you're expected. This will show that you value his or her time and it will ensure that you have a full meeting. If you will be late, contact him or her right away to apologize and let the instructor know. Offer to reschedule if it is more convenient for your instructor.

Avoid transition times. The times right before and right after class are usually not a good time to ask your instructor for assistance or guidance. Those transitions are not conducive to one-on-one conversations, as the instructor will probably be focused on getting materials together for class or talking with other students.

Come prepared. Carefully review the materials that have been presented in class. If you're going to ask for clarification or help, make sure you've done as much as possible to help yourself prior to the meeting. Bring your textbook and notes if necessary.

Difficulties with Instructors

You may encounter communication issues or other difficulties with instructors. These can be particularly frustrating your first year when you are establishing your independence and learning how to deal with conflict on your own. Here are the most common frustrations students have with instructors and ways of dealing with them:

Frustration #1:
I don't understand the material!
Make an appointment to talk with your instructor. In the meeting, ask specific questions rather than asking for general help. (*What made Piaget's use of psychometrics revolutionary?* rather than *Why is Piaget important?* and never *Now, what's a Piaget?*) Bring materials like homework assignments or notes to show that you have attempted to learn the material on your own. Listen and take notes.

Frustration #2:

I understand the material but my grade doesn't show it!

Make an appointment to talk with your instructor. First, make sure that you do in fact understand the material by showing some of your work and explaining your understanding of key concepts. This will give your instructor a chance to confirm you know your stuff or to tell you that you aren't actually mastering it the way you thought you were. If your grades don't reflect your knowledge, ask for ideas for how to perform better on exams and papers. Usually instructors are happy to work with interested students. Offer up your own solutions to a problem. Professors often appreciate forward thinking.

Frustration #3:

My instructor and I can't communicate!

Sometimes you run into someone who seems to speak another language—we mean this metaphorically, though of course it could be a literal statement. If you and your instructor have poor communication or a negative relationship, try contacting other students who have taken courses from him or her and ask for their recommendations on how to work with him or her. If one of you has offended the other, make an appointment and do your part to clear up any confusion.

Frustration #4:

I don't have difficulties with my instructor—I have a difficult instructor!

If you believe you've done everything you can to have a neutral to positive relationship with your instructor and nothing has worked, contact your academic advisor or college counselor for assistance and advice.

Developing Relationships with Your Classmates

Later in life you may have to rack your brain to think of topics of conversation when you're in a roomful of strangers. But in college you can look around at the other seven or fifty-two or four hundred students and know you have countless things in common and therefore an abundance of conversation topics. The latest reading. The most recent assignment. The last lecture. The upcoming exam. A related play or performance. Other classes. Coffee—where to get it, how much you need it, and how much you'd pay to have a cup of it materialize in your hands at this very instant. You get the picture.

It's relatively easy to meet the people around you and to strike up a simple conversation. Even in large lecture halls many people end up sitting in the same sections each class period, so it's a good chance you'll run into the same students on a regular basis. Build connections with other students during the transition times (the minutes before and after class) by engaging in conversation, asking questions, and comparing notes or ideas. Join field trips and other excursions that your instructor might offer; not only is it fun to learn outside the classroom, it's also an informal environment conducive to developing peer relationships.

Finally, collaborate with other students: create a study group or join one that's already formed, work on a group project if that's an option, and share ideas.

Developing Relationships in the Online Learning Environment

Some of your classes may have an online component and some may be entirely online. Developing relationships with your online instructor or classmates will make such classes richer and more rewarding. In many cases, the instructor will facilitate community building by requiring a certain number of posts or other online interactions. If possible, go beyond the requirements: get involved in the online discussions, reach out to classmates to create teams or study groups, and share interesting ideas and information that is relevant to the class material. Put your military leadership experience to good use by initiating conversations and encouraging a healthy flow of communication.

Consider This ...

After returning from my deployment in support of Operation Iraqi Freedom, I had a renewed sense of purpose. I had realized that I wanted to pursue a degree in social work, and was later accepted to one of the nation's top programs. I began classes less than a year after I came home.

Military themes were common in our social policy courses. I let it be known that I was a veteran, and suddenly I found my peers and instructors turning to me when controversial issues arose; pressing for reasons why tragic events occur in war zones, and seemingly wonder how I could support an organization that engages in such acts. Any time a news outlet posted an adverse article about the service, I was asked for comment. I felt like my instructors and peers looked at me as a spokesperson to explain things I took no part in, or events I was completely isolated from.

Despite my initial frustrations, I forced myself to acknowledge that I was among individuals who had limited knowledge and experience of military culture and combat environments. I took the opportunity to provide education on the stigma and misperceptions commonly attributed to the veteran population. Over time, I grew to appreciate their curiosity, because it meant they had a desire to understand, which eventually forged a connection between me and my civilian peers.

Geri Young, Air Force Veteran

Developing Relationships **Exercises**

1. What qualities does a great instructor possess? List as many as possible.

2. Think of teachers you've had in the past who were great but whose teaching style was very different from what usually works best for you. What made those teachers great?

3. What expectations do college instructors have of their students that are different from the expectations high school teachers have of their students? Brainstorm with another student and/or interview upperclassmen and/or instructors to answer this question.

4. Draw or describe in writing your vision of the ideal student-instructor-classmates relationship. Where do teaching, learning, and knowledge fit into your drawing or depiction?

5. Interview a classmate and introduce him or her to the class. Create interesting interview questions so other students will really get to know your subject. Introduce him or her in a memorable way.

Visit **www.LifeDuringCollege.com**
for more resources and exercises.

Learning Styles

CHAPTER 7

Hollywood's vision of learning includes agonizingly dull lectures (think *Ferris Bueller's Day Off*: the economics teacher intones, "The Hawley-Smoot Tariff Act, which…anyone?….Raised or lowered? ….Did it work?...anyone?") as well as inspiring classrooms where passionate teachers shout, "Stand up! Stand on your desks!" The teacher either numbs or transforms. The students are either stunned by boredom or awestruck. What's missing from many of these fictional versions of school is the students' active role in their own self-transformations.

You will have inspiring, passionate instructors, but don't wait for someone to leap onto a desk and recite poetry. You are your most important teacher. A successful student knows that and knows how to learn. He or she is open to new ideas, engages with and reflects on his or her experiences, and seeks challenges. In this chapter we'll

> *When the student is ready, the master will appear.*
> **Buddhist Proverb**

- provide a brief overview of the learning process

- give examples of individual learning styles and complementary study strategies

- discuss the importance of being an active learner and a critical thinker

The Learning Process

What is learning? Definitions of learning abound and sometimes contradict each other. There are theories, charts, seemingly paradoxical explanations ("learning is the act of unlearning"), models and wikis.

We'll keep it simple here and focus on one widely used and referenced definition, and suggest resources if you'd like information about others. Learning is, according to David Kolb, a professor at Case Western Reserve University and an influential educational theorist, "the process whereby knowledge is created through the transformation of experience. Knowledge results from the combination of grasping and transforming experience." Kolb's model of experiential learning involves action and reflection, experience and abstraction. Students may process information differently and prefer one mode over another, but the best learning occurs when students—and instructors—integrate all four modes. Here is an adaptation of the learning construct Kolb describes.

ACTION	REFLECTION
Learn by doing. **Put theories to the test, relate concepts in your own way.** Examples: Papers, projects, creating models	**Learn by thinking about what you've heard, seen, experienced, etc.** Examples: Discussions, journaling, brainstorming
EXPERIENCE	ABSTRACTION
Learn through direct involvement. Examples: Field work, labs, simulations, homework	**Learn by observing and reading.** Examples: Attending lectures, reading the textbook, thinking about concepts

Successful students involve themselves in concrete experiences, reflect on their experiences (reflection), create concepts and theories based on their reflections (abstraction), then test those theories (action). Learning, then, is a process and each step builds on the previous one. People don't necessarily learn in a specific order—some move from abstraction to action, for example—and many students exhibit a preference for one of these modes of learning.

Which category or categories seem like a good match for you? When you bring home a bookshelf from IKEA, are you more likely to take all the pieces out and get right to work (action) or read the directions thoroughly (abstraction) before you even consider picking up that little hex key? After wrestling the new bookshelf into place, will you reflect on the experience? (Hmm, maybe next time I should wait for my roommate to help me!)

Discovering Your Learning Style

If you're interested in identifying and exploring your learning or personality type, there are plenty of resources to assist you. They range from long, detailed inventories to quick questionnaires. These tools can help you articulate your strengths and weaknesses, give you insights into how you relate to other people, and suggest majors and professions that might spark your interest and play to your strengths. However, you should also know that there is much debate in the education community about the validity of categorizing learning styles. That said, we'll share one popular model with you for your information—and leave it up to you to decide how helpful it might be.

One popular model of learning styles proposes that people prefer learning through visual, auditory, or tactile/kinesthetic modes. For example, a visual learner might be more likely to retain information from class when it is presented with film and images. A visual learner might need to sketch out a concept in order to understand it, and would benefit from using color-coded notes and flash cards. A tactile/kinesthetic learner, on the other hand, might learn more from hands-on activities and labs, and could use rhythm to help him or her memorize information.

You probably already know quite a bit about how you learn and have discovered from experience that what works for you doesn't always work for other people. Take a look at the following table. Which characteristics do you recognize in yourself? Are you more of a visual learner, an auditory learner, a tactile/kinesthetic learner, or are you a combination of learning types? What can you add to the "Learns Best From" column? Which of the recommended learning strategies have you already tried? Which ones work best for you? Which ones will you try?

	Characteristics	Learns Best From	Learning Strategies
Visual Learner	• Learns by seeing • Thinks in pictures • Prefers written directions • Draws ideas on paper • Remembers faces • Imagines scenes and characters in books • Seeks out pictures and graphs to understand material • May not retain auditory information for long	• Lectures with images • Diagrams, charts • Pictures • Films	• Write out notes and lists • Create pictures and diagrams to understand and retain information • Use graphic organizers • Color code notes and study guides • Make and use flashcards
Auditory Learner	• Learns by hearing/talking • Attentive to discussions • Prefers verbal directions • Remembers names • Sensitive to intonation, pitch, and tone of voice • May be distracted by noise	• Lectures • Discussions • Presentations and speeches	• Read explanations, directions, and study notes out loud • Form study groups and discuss class material • Use audio books • Create rhymes and songs to help remember material • Record lectures and review them
Tactile/Kines-thetic Learner	• Learns by doing/feeling • Expresses self through movement and gesture • Remembers activities • Prefers to experiment, figure things out • May have difficulties reading and spelling	• Hands-on activities • Experiments and lab work • Skits, role-plays, and performances	• Use rhythm to memorize information (e.g., pace while reviewing flash cards) • Create models of concepts and information • Make and use flashcards • Visualize using physical sensation cues

Learning Style & Personality Type Surveys

GOOD TO KNOW

Discover yourself (and put off writing that research paper)!

Kolb Learning Style Inventory

Learning and Study Strategies Inventory (LASSI)

VARK Learning Style Inventory

Multiple Intelligence Inventory

Myers-Briggs Type Indicator (MBTI)

These are just some of the popular learning style and personality type surveys. A few are available online; others may be available through your college's career or counseling office.

Active Learning and Critical Thinking

More important than your preferred learning style and your dominant personality traits is whether you are an active learner. Here we mean cognitively active rather than jumping-jacks-in-the-lecture-hall active. Do you ask questions, either out loud in class or internally as you read? Do you anticipate outcomes? Do you propose theories? Do you follow your curiosity? Do you reflect on your understanding of a topic and identify gaps in your knowledge? Do you look for biases in your own thinking and in others'? Do you synthesize new information with previous knowledge? The active learner does all of these things all of the time. In fact, the term "active learner" is redundant: A learner does all these things all the time.

The passive learner, by contrast, simply consumes information. To the passive learner, a lecture is like a TV show, and a lab is just a series of actions one must imitate. The term "passive learner," then, is a misnomer, as there is no real learning taking place in these examples.

One of the hallmarks of an active learner is the ability to **think critically**. According to Edward Glaser, co-author of the *Watson-Glaser Critical Thinking Appraisal* (1941), critical thinking requires a certain attitude, a body of knowledge, and skills:

Attitude: The critical thinker considers ideas and information in a thoughtful way. The word consider comes from the Latin *considerare*, meaning "to inspect closely, to observe." A critical thinker's attitude, then, is being observant and ready to inspect.

Knowledge: The critical thinker possesses knowledge of the methods of logical inquiry and reasoning. She or he understands how to approach his or her own or another person's argument systematically and with established criteria.

Skills: The critical thinker knows how and when to apply her or his knowledge and does so skillfully.

The Critical Thinker

- Pays attention
- Considers the argument
- Challenges assumptions (including his or her own)
- Asks questions
- Recognizes claims and facts
- Examines the evidence
- Understands the difference between reason and faulty reasoning

Note that when we talk about critical thinking, there are two frequently misconstrued terms. First, the word *critical* often connotes "judging harshly," as in "Hannah was so critical of the restaurant that we couldn't even mention it in her presence." But a critical thinker will think critically about everything, whether he or she loves, hates, or feels neutral about it. Second, the word *argument* often connotes disagreement, especially a verbal disagreement. *Argument* in the academic sense means "a course of reasoning."

College is the place to hone your critical thinking skills and to master the art of active learning, so if some of this is new you're in the right place!

Learning Styles **Exercises**

1. Consider each of your classes. What types of action, reflection, experience, and abstraction do they incorporate? What can you do to integrate the four modes of learning in each class?

2. Do you consider yourself more of a visual, auditory, or tactile/kinesthetic learner? Which learning strategies have you tried that fit your learning style well? What new learning strategies will you try this term?

3. Take a learning style and/or personality inventory. Your instructor or the college counseling center may recommend one or you can go online and complete one of the inventories mentioned in this chapter.

Visit **www.LifeDuringCollege.com** for more resources and exercises.

Memory Skills & Multitasking

CHAPTER 8

Now for a test: In what year did Columbus sail the ocean blue? How many days hath September? What percentage of our brains do we actually use?

The answers are 1492, 30, and 100%.

How did you do? Many people would get the first two correct and the last one wrong. When something is stored in the brain and we can retrieve it easily—through a rhyme or because we have a strong association, for instance—it is an indelible memory. If you answered 10% to the last question you remembered correctly, but remembered a myth. The 10% myth is often repeated in our culture in ads and everyday conversations, and it's usually attributed to an authority, such as Albert Einstein. It's also believable: I must be using only 10% of my brain; otherwise, I would have remembered to turn off the stove/pay the bill/make that appointment. No wonder so many of us have locked it away as a memory. In order to remember that it's a myth we'll have to make a concerted effort to relearn or "unlearn" our prior knowledge.

Memory is not the same thing as learning. A person who remembers all sorts of facts, dates, and information but does not understand their context is not knowledgeable. A wise person understands concepts, analyzes and synthesizes ideas, and thinks critically—and knows that learning is not simply accruing bits of information. However, strengthening your memory will help you do well at college, so in this chapter we will

- define short-term and long-term memory
- discuss the factors that support building memory
- provide memorization tips and tricks
- discuss multitasking and how it inhibits concentration

Short-term and Long-term Memory

Learning literally changes your brain: It changes the internal structure of neurons and increases the number of synapses between neurons. Memory is the record of the learning process.

Short-term memory is a temporary record. Most people's brains hold only about seven units of information for a few dozen seconds. You can capitalize on your short term memory by "chunking" information. Let's say you need to remember this number: 578206781. The task would exhaust your seven units of storage space unless you "chunk" the digits into groups. In this case, you could divide it into three chunks, like a social security number: 578   20 6781. By chunking the information and repeating it you can stretch the capacity of your short-term memory.

Long-term memory includes memory of recent facts (if you can remember the three questions at the beginning of this section, they are technically in your long-term memory) as well as older, consolidated information. There are three processes involved in establishing a long term memory: encoding, storage, and retrieval.

1) To encode, you assign meaning to the information. Let's say you wanted to remember the meaning of the word "monopoly." You might encode it by associating the word and its meaning with the board game Monopoly.

> **Want to know more about the brain, learning, and memory?** *TIP*
>
> Check out the Canadian Institute of Neuroscience, Mental Health, and Addiction's website: *The Brain From Top to Bottom* http://thebrain.mcgill.ca/

You could encode it further by breaking the word into its root meanings: *mono* = "alone" and *pol* = "to sell." You could picture your sister monopolizing a conversation. You could assign it emotional or sensory significance (for example, imagining the word written in a certain color).

2) To store the word, you would review it and its meanings. (In other words, study.) Also, get some sleep. Research suggests that sleep plays a significant role in consolidating information.

3) To retrieve it, you follow the path you laid for yourself through encoding. *Monopoly*, hmm, it's like the board game and it reminds me of a certain company, I can see the word written in big steel-colored letters, I can hear my sister jabbering on and on…Ah! *Monopoly* is to have complete control over something!

Remember the story of Hansel and Gretel, the children who went for a walk in the woods and scattered breadcrumbs behind them so they could find their way home later? Animals ate up their breadcrumbs and they were stuck with a wicked witch in a freaky gingerbread cottage. The moral of the story? Don't encode with breadcrumbs. You want something nice and lasting to help you find your way back to your stored memory.

Some long-term memories don't require deliberate encoding and storing: Your first kiss, a traumatic event, the smell of a favorite place. People can recall in great detail where they were and what they were doing on the morning of September 11th, 2001 because the shock of the events of that morning was so great.

Much of what you read, hear, and view in college, however, won't necessarily be intense. Therefore, you will need to make a concerted effort to learn and remember. Here are four factors that influence memory:

Attentiveness: Concentrate on the information.

Motivation: Decide why you want to remember the information. Sometimes this will come naturally. For example, you've probably forgotten the number we used in the "chunking" explanation earlier in this section because you recognized there was no motivation to remember it. In other cases you'll need to determine the purpose and worth of the information.

> **Memory Retrieval: Recognize or Recall?**
>
> *Good To Know*
>
> Are you remembering in order to recognize information or recall it? To recognize something is to know it at a superficial level. Multiple choice and matching tests generally assess your ability to recognize correct answers or to use process of elimination to rule out incorrect answers. Recall suggests deeper understanding of the material.

Emotional state: Remembering your emotional state when you first took in the information can help retrieve it. Also, some emotional states are more conducive to encoding memories than others. If you're anxious and stressed about finals week you might retain a strong memory of your emotional state but have a hard time remembering the course content you need to master.

Context (sights, sounds, smells, place): Connecting the information to sensation, location, or other contextual clues will help you encode it.

You can improve your ability to remember information by incorporating these factors into your daily practice. Your participation in class, note taking, and regular study habits should all help strengthen your memory retention and learning.

Memorization Tips & Tricks

Once you're motivated to memorize material, try these tips and tricks:

Break it down: Memorize sections at a time. Take in new information piece by piece and rehearse as you go—it's less overwhelming than trying to remember the whole thing at once and it's more likely the content will make more sense when you master it bit by bit.

Organize it: What's most important? Which comes first, which last? Is one person, idea, or event dependent on another? What are the relationships between elements? Drawing a graphic organizer can help you understand the material better and retain it, too.

Practice it: Write it, recite it, work with it. The repetition builds the pathways you need to store the information in your long term memory.

Move it: Kinesthetic practice works for a lot of people. This can range from simply pacing while reading to choreographing memory hooks with facial expressions and body movements. The drawback of this method: Your roommate might think you've gone crazy. The benefit: You remember the information.

Overemphasize it: Too much of a concept or fact is sometimes just enough to retain it. When studying vocabulary, for instance, you could try using your newest words in many more situations than you normally would. ("Oh, thank you! That's so *perspicacious* of you! Do you think he's *perspicacious*? If I were more *perspicacious* I would have noticed that..." OK, OK, you get the point. Because you're *perspicacious*....)

Teach it: One way to ensure you've mastered material is to teach it to somebody else. Put it into your own words. Explain it. Draw it out for someone who is not familiar with the material. Anticipate questions a person might have about the topic and be prepared to answer them.

Use mnemonics. Mnemonics are memory tools that help you encode and retrieve information. Songs ("Fifty, nifty United States..."), rhymes ("I before E except after C..."), acronyms, and imagery are powerful ways to remember. Try including sensations in your imagery.

Test it: You want to recall the information in a variety of situations. Reading a page of notes over and over is not going to help most people retain the information. Flashcards–or other means of splitting questions and answers, terms and definitions–are great for this because they force you to come up with the answer.

Your memory skills support all the other academic skills, so we'll come back to some of the terms and ideas from this section. Before we move on to reading, writing, and the other skills, we need to switch gears, interrupt this topic, take just a second, to talk about...hold on, let me pick up this call...multitasking.

The Case Against Multitasking

Memory depends on concentration. Multitasking interrupts concentration. It inhibits learning and productivity. In his book *CrazyBusy*, psychiatrist Dr. Edward Hallowell defines multitasking as "a mythical activity in which people believe they can perform two or more tasks simultaneously."

The word multitasking itself is misleading, as research has consistently found that the brain does not have the capacity for focusing on many things at once. Instead, it switches among tasks. Focus. Switch. Focus. Switch. The result is a loss of focus, loss of productivity and, often, an increase in stress. Frequent multitaskers think they are exceptions, that they somehow have mastered the art of managing multiple tasks and information streams. Brain scans and other tests show otherwise. In an interview on National Public Radio, Professor Earl Miller, a neuroscientist at MIT, said, "Switching from task to task, you think you're actually paying attention to everything around you at the same time. But you're actually not." In fact, those who think they are the best at multitasking are, in Miller's words, "deluding themselves."

In 2005, Dr. Glenn Wilson of the University of London conducted a study for Hewlett-Packard on the effects of multitasking. He found that workers distracted by email and phone calls experience a 10-point drop in IQ points—more than twice the impact of smoking marijuana or losing a night's sleep. It's not a permanent drop, but it's still counterproductive.

What about listening to music while studying? In this case, studies support what some students already knew: the brain can effectively block out or "quiet" white noise and music while focusing on a more challenging task, such as memorizing geologic features or learning a chemistry equation. For many people, background noise stays in the background and doesn't compete with the more demanding stuff at hand.

How to break the multitasking habit:

Become conscious of your multitasking. How often do you check social media while writing a paper? How frequently do you respond to interruptions such as texts and phone messages?

Set reasonable goals, e.g., "I will turn off my phone for one hour while I finish this math set."

Make it possible. Remove or limit distractions or, conversely, remove yourself from distracting situations. Roommates, your computer, the refrigerator—you know the worst (or favorite?) interruptions and can figure out ways to avoid them. For instance, some people choose to self-monitor time spent on certain websites; services such as minutesplease.com allow users to set time limits on distracting websites.

Reward yourself for focusing on one task at a time, e.g., "When I am satisfied I understand these equations I can check Twitter."

We realize that some of you are still not convinced. No amount of research or number of brain scans will persuade you that multitasking negatively affects learning and concentration. But there's nothing to lose from trying some of the above tips—and a lot to gain if at least one of them helps you focus and work more productively.

Memory Skills and Multitasking **Exercises**

1. Describe a test you've taken recently that tested your ability to recognize information. How did you study for it? How did you do on it? What are the benefits and drawbacks of these kinds of tests?

2. Now describe a test you've taken recently that tested your ability to recall information. How did you study for it? How did you do on it? What are the benefits and drawbacks of these kinds of tests?

3. With a partner, create an exam for this chapter (or another chapter in this book) that tests students' abilities to recognize or recall information. Switch exams with another pair of students. After all parties have taken an exam and graded it, discuss the process: To what extent did preparing a test help you remember the material? What were the best questions and prompts? Why?

4. Multitasking Log. Challenge yourself: What's the longest you can focus on a single school-related task, such as reading, studying, writing, researching, or working in the lab? The next time you're working on a school-related task, keep track of the number of minutes you spend on task versus the number of minutes you spend off task (checking social media, getting a snack, picking out the perfect music to accompany your work, etc.) Write 1 – 2 paragraphs that reflect on what you learned about your own multitasking and/or the interruptions you encounter.

Visit **www.LifeDuringCollege.com**
for more resources and exercises.

Communication, Note Taking & Study Skills

CHAPTER 9

It's not what you know that's important, but how you know it and how well you communicate it to others. Whether you're majoring in Anthrozoology or Japanese, you need to master the same essential skills: How to learn and how to communicate. The best students (and graduates, for that matter) can write and present well. They participate in class, take good notes, and study effectively. This chapter will help you become not just a successful student, but a master student. It will

- provide an overview of the writing process

- outline the critical reading, writing, and speaking skills

- explain the importance of participation and give you strategies for participating in a meaningful way

- provide essential tips for note taking and studying

- identify resources that will help you master your studies

The Writing Process - Thinking About Your Thinking

One crucial thing to remember before you write any paper: Writing is a part of a larger process and the vehicle by which you express your ideas. When you write a paper you want to go beyond providing a simple regurgitation of the material. Sit with what you have read, go through your lecture notes, and think about how these things challenge or support ideas that you already have. Thinking about your thinking, researching and reading, taking notes, deciding what to include and what to exclude, developing an outline, and revising and editing will refine your ideas into a thoughtful and concise paper. Expect to end up with a different product than you aimed for. That's how you progress.

Here's a general overview of the writing process:

1. Pre-write. The tasks: identify an interesting topic, determine the position you'll take in the paper, brainstorm ideas, develop an outline, research, read, and gather evidence. If your instructor has provided a rubric, read over it carefully at this stage of the writing process. Rubrics are designed to give students a clear writing target; in other words, they show you exactly what your instructor will consider when he or she evaluates your paper. If time allows, ask for feedback on your outline from a friend or tutor.

2. Write. The tasks: Develop a thesis statement, a conclusion, write the body paragraphs, and craft an introduction.

3. Revise. The tasks: Review your first draft with a critical eye, revise it, and then proofread it.

Here we'll add a step missing from the popular model of the writing process:

4. Reflect. The tasks: After your instructor returns your paper, reread it and any comments he or she made. Keep a critical distance from your own work so you can fairly appraise its strengths and weaknesses. Use any feedback you get to inform the way you write your next paper.

Some words of advice: **Stay flexible** throughout the process and you'll end up with a better paper. For instance, **expect your thesis to change** and develop as you write. With research papers, expect to keep researching in the latter stages of the writing process. Also, **take notes on your readings and sources** as you go so that you won't have to backtrack or, even worse, get stuck without proper records of your sources.

Writing Skills

Professors have observed a steady decline in college students' basic writing skills. All students—including math and science majors—need to know how to write well in a variety of contexts. If a student hasn't mastered the basics before college, he or she should seek remediation even before he or she unpacks the new mini-fridge. Colleges usually provide entry-level composition classes, workshops and specialized sessions on writing, in addition to well-staffed writing centers. Some schools, like Purdue University, have top-notch online writing resources—which can be particularly helpful if you're working on a paper at 3 a.m., when no tutoring centers are open. You can help yourself by taking advantage of these resources and learning the essentials of good writing.

> *I never write* Metropolis *for seven cents because I can get the same price for* city. *I never write* policeman *because I can get the same money for* cop.
>
> **Mark Twain,**
> **American author and humorist**

Whether you're writing for a science class or an English class, good writing has clarity, focus, voice, fluency, and follows the rules of standard conventions.

Clarity
Be clear and specific. Use precise language, not overblown verbiage or filler material. Edit out any ambiguities or awkward sections.

To check for clarity:

- **Take a break.** Come back to your paper with fresh eyes.

- **Read it aloud.** Listen to the meaning and rhythm of each sentence, as well as to the way the sentences work together.

- **Make sure the style is consistent.** Common inconsistencies include shifting verb tenses and nouns/pronouns (*people* shifts to *a person* or *one* or *everybody* or *you*)

- **Don't use jargon.** Avoid vocabulary words you don't fully understand or don't need.

- **Kill the filler.** Read the paper again, this time looking for fluff or filler material. Frequent fillers: adverbs (Examples: *It was a(n) ~~incredibly~~ rich experience. I ~~sincerely~~ hope you'll respond.*); redundancies (*At this ~~point in time~~.... It was a ~~very~~ unique opportunity*); and general wordiness (*Seeing as though she was wanting a change*.... or *Despite the fact that Harriet was wanting a change for the better*... becomes, simply, *Harriet wanted a change.*)

Focus

Your reader should be able to follow your thoughts from a compelling introduction, through logically organized ideas in the body paragraphs, to a resounding conclusion. Hypothetically, a reader should be able to pick up random sections of your essay and piece them back together in the correct order. How? Because the argument will flow from one idea to the next, you'll have used transition words to signal shifts in ideas or topics, and there will be nothing extraneous to distract from your ideas. Another, more likely, test is if another classmate or your professor could read your paper, then easily respond to the questions, "What is this paper about? What are the author's main ideas?"

To check for focus:

- **Take a break.** Come back to your paper with fresh eyes.

- **Check your thesis statement.** Is it clear, specific, and arguable? Do the ideas in the rest of the paper spring from it?

- **Identify the main idea in each paragraph.** This is usually the topic sentence. Each sentence in the paragraph should connect in some way to the topic sentence. If a sentence doesn't connect, it needs to go, no matter how attached you are to it.

- **Ensure each paragraph is distinct.** If you find yourself restating ideas and even quoting the same material in different paragraphs, that's a sign that you need to pull all of that related material into the same paragraph and cut the rest.

- **Ask a friend to review your paper.** If your friend can restate your thesis and main ideas, you've succeeded. If your friend is confused by parts of it, go back to the paper and rework it until it will pass this test.

Voice

Or, more appropriately, control of voice. Know your audience, purpose, and topic, and write accordingly. Your voice will vary depending on your audience and purpose. The tone you take should be intentional and effective.

To check for voice:

- **Reread the paper out loud.** Ask yourself, *Is there a clear audience, purpose, and topic?* and *Is the tone consistent and appropriate to the audience, purpose, and topic?*

Fluency

You want your reader, whether it's a professor, a teaching assistant, or a classmate, to pause only to reflect on your insights and ideas. You want them to think, "Ah!" and "Hmm, I hadn't thought of that!" not "What?" or "How much longer must I endure?" Fluency is how the paper flows. It should move naturally from one idea to the next. Your sentence structure and word choice should highlight your ideas, not distract from them.

To check for fluency:

- **Take a break.** Come back to your paper with fresh eyes.

- **Check the introduction and conclusion.** Are they compelling? Clearly connected to the topic explored in your paper?

- **Identify transition words and phrases.** Make sure you smoothly transition between each body paragraph or between sentences within a paragraph.

- **Check for common sentence structure errors**, including run-ons, comma splices, and fragments.

Mastery of Conventions

If you're a phonetic speller or an inveterate comma splicer, now is the time to kick the habit. Conventions should not be noticeable to your reader; if you've mastered them, no one will say, "Wow, excellent use of the semicolon!" or, "I love how her pronouns always agree with their antecedents!" If you haven't mastered them they will distract from your ideas.

To check for conventions:

- **Give yourself time.** Make sure you have enough time between the paper's final printing and its due date to go over it and look for errors in spelling, punctuation, and grammar.

- **Find fresh eyes.** Ask a friend or tutor at the writing center to proofread your paper.

Public Speaking Skills

The ability to communicate effectively is a core part of the college experience and an invaluable tool for your career. Looking back on your service, you likely participated in different types of communication that ranged from daily operational briefings to formal change of command ceremonies. Maybe you were so skilled in your MOS that you were the go-to person who provided training to the platoon or the NCO who read award citations to deserving members of your unit. Although the prospect of speaking publically and giving presentations in college may seem intimidating, chances are you are already more seasoned than you realize.

Many schools have speaking labs, similar to writing centers. Speaking labs are staffed with people trained to assist students in preparing for public speaking and video presentations. They often offer one-on-one assistance as well as all the necessary equipment and technology.

The public speaking you do will vary depending on your area of study, but most likely will include the following types: Impromptu speaking, presentations, and speeches.

Impromptu speaking is in class and on the spot, hence the most informal of the types of public speaking. Your preparation for speaking in these cases will be minimal. That is, you'll have read the material and prepared for class, but you probably won't have speaking notes. Here are some tips for responding to questions and sharing ideas on the spot in class:

- **Listen well.** Your classmates' and instructors' ideas will inform your own. When you listen carefully, you'll be able to add meaningfully to the discussion. Also, you'll be less likely to be caught off guard if your professor calls on you. If your instructor does call on you and you don't fully understand her or his question (or if your attention was wandering), rephrase the question in your own words or ask him or her to repeat it.

- **State your opinion.** In the course of a discussion, your opinion will change and develop, so state your opinion as it is in that moment.

- **Explain your reasoning.** Why do you think the way you do? What evidence supports your opinion? Anticipate these questions and use them to develop your point.

- **Show respect.** Acknowledge the validity of previous speakers even if you disagree with their arguments. Restate what you hear and use "I" statements. Example: "I agree with Travis's point about the Supreme Court's decision. However, I see it from a different angle...."

Presentations, informal and formal, are often required in college classes. To give successful individual or group presentations,

- **Define your audience and purpose.** A persuasive presentation for a small group of faculty and students requires a different style than an entertaining presentation for a group of peers.

- **Put content first.** Before you think about visual layout and other style considerations, decide what you want to say, how you want to say it, and what you want your audience to take away from your presentation.

- **Keep it lean.** Get your audience's attention at the very beginning and make sure each subsequent part of the presentation gives them something valuable, whether it's information or entertainment.

- **Keep it clean.** Stay focused on your topic and make sure your visuals add to your presentation without cluttering it. Visuals should support the content, not be the content. If you're tempted to read the text on your PowerPoint to the audience, that's a clue that the slides are too text-heavy.

- **Make visuals visible.** Choose appealing colors and make sure text, images, and charts are large enough for the audience to see easily. Use bullet points and spare text. You want the slides and/or images to emphasize what you say, not take over.

- **Be the presenter.** This seems obvious, but sometimes students will spend weeks creating a PowerPoint presentation, then stand in front of the class on the day of the presentation and let the slides do all the work. Or, some students will back off too much when a co-presenter is speaking and become merely an observer.

- **Face your audience.** Make eye contact with people in all sections of the room, not just the instructor. If you need to write on your flip chart or smart board during your presentation, pause and then resume speaking.

- **Practice.** Practice your delivery and practice with any technology you're using so you'll feel confident on the day of the presentation.

Presentations ultimately depend on knowledge and preparation. No number of quirky slide transitions or funny YouTube clips can cover weak content.

The process of organizing a presentation with a group usually takes longer and involves more discussion of each step; however, the collaboration can be fruitful if the group members are committed to doing a good job. If you are assigned a group presentation project, try to meet up with your group members as soon as possible so you can map out a plan and preparation schedule that allows all group members to participate fully.

Often, instructors will assign group projects that include a presentation component. In such cases, the presentation is usually worth a big percentage of the overall grade, yet groups often fail to plan well for it. Make sure that you and your group members spend an adequate amount of time preparing for presentations.

Speeches are usually the most formal (and, for some students, the most anxiety-producing) of the three types of public speaking, though some professors will require extemporaneous (spur of the moment) speeches. Here are some tips for writing and presenting a speech:

- **Define your audience and purpose.** An oral presentation needs to be laser-beam focused in order to keep your audience engaged.

- **Prepare your message.** You'll need to start with a good hook, some compelling anecdote, question, statement, or even a joke that engages your audience right away. Decide on your main points and choose the best evidence to support those points. Decide to what extent you want to appeal to your audience's emotions or logic. Make sure your conclusion is clear and effective.

- **Edit.** Once you have a draft, read it out loud at a good public speaking pace several times to hear the rhythm and the message. A good public speaking pace is slower than conversational speech. Read it to a friend and ask him or her to reflect what he or she hears: Are the main points clearly stated? Are transitions between ideas easy to follow? Edit based on any feedback you get.

- **Practice.** Read aloud, first with the entire text in front of you, but later with just those notes you'll have on the day of the actual speech. If you can, film yourself so you can watch your delivery and make changes as needed. Watching yourself on film might not be the most enjoyable way to spend an afternoon, but it will definitely make you aware of any quirks that need to change.

- **Know the rules of good delivery.** Speak loudly and clearly enough to be heard in all corners of the room. Vary your speaking rate (pace), pitch, and volume to keep your audience engaged and to emphasize certain points. Use pauses. Avoid verbal clutter, such as "um" and "like." Practice making purposeful physical gestures that underscore your message. Make eye contact with audience members—not just the one who'll be grading you!

- **Use visuals and other media effectively.** Use only those parts of the film or audio clip that relate to your message. Make sure visuals are large and clear. Don't allow your media to replace your content.

These tips are just a starting point. Your professors will give you more specific information about what's expected in their classes and in their discipline.

How to Gain Confidence with Public Speaking

Good To Know

See each speech or presentation as an opportunity to improve and to overcome any anxiety you may have.

Assume that your audience wants you to do well. They do.

Know your stuff. Understand the content thoroughly, including any charts or graphs you'll share with your audience.

Practice your speech or presentation until it feels smooth, then practice some more. It's especially helpful to do a dry run in the location where you'll be speaking. If you can't access the same classroom or lecture hall, find a room that has similar dimensions so you can get used to the space and your own volume.

Concentrate on the content. Yes, your delivery is important, but your audience is there to hear your message. Focusing on the content while you're in front of the room will help you tune out any distracting or anxiety-producing thoughts you have.

Participation Skills

Like public speaking and writing, participation is a skill to develop and master. Participation is a bit different, however, because instructors don't always overtly insist on or evaluate it. But they all value student participation.

When you actively listen and respond to class discussions and lectures, you're not just demonstrating interest (which instructors love to see, of course!), you're actually activating your curiosity, which in turn leads to true learning. Finals week will be a lot less stressful if you participate fully in class every day because you'll remember the material better and you'll already understand it.

Here's what good participation looks like:

Be prepared. An OK student does the assigned work on time. A good participant completes the assigned work (and suggested readings, whenever possible) and notes questions she or he has about the material, or connections between the material and something else the class has studied. These notes may become in-class questions or comments.

Be there. Attend class regularly and on time and make it your focus for the hour or however long it lasts. Limit distractions for yourself. Turn off your phone and commit to using your laptop for notes only.

Sit in the front where your instructor will notice you and where you'll be more likely to stay engaged in the lecture or discussion.

Listen well. A good participant tracks the discussion and takes some notes on other students' questions and comments, as well as his own ideas and questions. Note taking during discussion helps you stay focused and interested. It also comes in handy when you're ready to speak because you'll be able to refer specifically to what others have said. You'll also have something to say.

Add to class discussions. Ideally, every student should add to a discussion; that's what makes a vibrant, interesting class. The ideal is not always reality, however. Sometimes classes are too big and the time too short to allow for everyone to have a voice. More often, a few students are superstar participants—or dominators—and the rest stay quiet, unwilling to break into the discussion. If you are the type to hold back, set some goals for participation so that you don't lose out on the learning opportunity. Even a goal of speaking once every other class is better than staying in the background for the term. If you are the type to speak up a lot, see what you can do to help balance the class discussions. You might need to hold back sometimes in order to let others add their voices. Or, you could try asking questions of other students to elicit their opinions on a subject.

Ask questions. Pursue your curiosity and interest. Also, ask questions of other students to facilitate a dynamic class discussion. As we mentioned in Chapter 6, it's best to avoid asking certain questions, such as "Is this going to be on the exam?" and "Did I miss anything?" In general, instructors want to engage students in learning, not simply to inform students how to perform for a grade.

Participate online. Many instructors require that students participate on listservs or online discussion groups. Such forums provide a great opportunity to those students who are shy or who need more time to formulate their ideas and questions. Your online participation should demonstrate insight, attention to detail, and true interaction with the other individuals involved in the discussion. Some students simply dash off their responses and comments online—and miss the opportunity for meaningful interaction, as well as a chance to improve their grade.

Participation is good for your learning and good for your grade. It's also one thing that can make or break a class. You could have the most engaging, interested professor doing academic cartwheels at the front of the room, but all of her or his efforts are for nothing if the students in class don't bring their own engaging, interested selves.

Note Taking Skills

This is one area that tends to separate the college student from the high school student in a big way. High school lecture classes are for good reason broader, slower, and more supportive than college lecture classes. Do you remember a high school teacher ever telling a student to take out her notes? Probably twelve times a class period, right? In college a professor is unlikely to remind anybody to do anything. Unlike high school teachers, college instructors are teaching adults who are paying a lot of money to attend classes. They assume their students know how to take notes and will do so if they're interested in doing well in class.

Of course you are interested in doing well. However, many first-year college students need tips on how to take notes effectively at the college level. Here are the basics you'll need to get started:

Why take notes?
It's possible to go through some classes without taking notes. The instructor or other students might post lecture notes online and instructors often hand out copies of their presentation slides. These are all helpful, but they won't necessarily accomplish the main objective, which is long-term learning. Being in class, actively listening and participating, and taking thoughtful notes will activate your brain and help you encode and store the information and concepts presented that day. Another reason to take good notes is that the printouts you receive do not usually contain all the information and ideas actually conveyed during the class period.

What is note taking?
It is not simply recording a lecture or chapter in writing. When you take notes you decide which ideas are important enough to write down, how they should be organized, and which examples best illustrate them.

What are effective notes?
They identify the main ideas of a lecture or text, identify pertinent supporting details, and are organized and arranged in a way that enhances your understanding of the material at the time and later, when you're studying for the test.

How do you take good notes?

Note taking is a skill and an art. You'll develop your own system eventually. In the meantime, here are four note taking formats to consider:

1) The Formal Outline. This format looks just like you'd expect a formal outline to look: Roman numerals denoting key ideas, other ideas represented by uppercase letters, etc. In essence, you recreate your presenter's outline for her lecture.

2) The Paragraph or List Format. These are similar systems that entail summarizing the key points and supporting details. The list format is distinct because it has more bullet points and indentations to separate information.

3) The Cornell Format. This popular format adds a study helper to the formats listed above. Draw a vertical line about 2 ½ inches from the left edge of your paper: this will be your "cue" column. At the bottom of the page, about 1 ½ inches from the bottom edge, draw a horizontal line: this will be your summary space.

In the right-hand column write your notes as you listen to a lecture or read a text. As soon as you can after class, write in the cue column questions and main ideas that relate to the material in the right-hand column. In the space at the bottom, summarize the notes on that page. The Cornell Format is a great way to review material. The split columns are also a ready-made study guide, as you can easily cover one side up and test yourself.

4) The Mind Map. Some students prefer the mind map method, where a central idea sprouts "branches" of related ideas and details. This enables one to visualize how concepts are related to each other. The mind map is better for notes on texts than lectures.

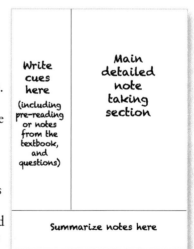

FORMAL OUTLINE

I Subject Item One

   A. Relevant info or description

   B. More info

II Subject Item Two

   A. Relevant info or description

   C. More info

   D. Etc.

CORNELL FORMAT

Write cues here (including pre-reading or notes from the textbook, and questions)

Main detailed note taking section

Summarize notes here

5) Question, Quote, or Comment (QQC). One technique that students find helpful, particularly when there is a lot of assigned reading, is the QQC. With the exception of a few lucky individuals, most of us can only retain a limited amount of information. A QQC is a handy tool for focusing on what you feel are the key points of a reading. For example, imagine you are assigned to read a 20-page article. Instead of trying to sift through everything the author mentions, focus on identifying a question, quote, or comment that arose from the reading. This may be something that piqued your interest, a powerful statement that grabbed you, or a general comment that you're still considering. QQC is a great way to identify the "deliverables" that you plan to share with the class. Other things to keep in mind about note taking:

Print out PowerPoint slides in advance. Many professors make their lectures available online before the class period. Whenever possible, print out and preview the lecture notes and slides so that you'll be prepared for class. Doing so will also ensure that you don't waste time taking unnecessary notes during class.

Use abbreviations. You can't possibly write everything down—nor should you—but it will help to keep up with your instructor if you use abbreviations whenever possible.

Review your lecture notes soon after class, preferably by the end of the day. Don't wait until the end of the semester to pull them out and study. Reviewing them right away will ensure that you remember the material. Also, you'll be able to see where you have gaps in knowledge—and formulate questions for the instructor the next day.

Keep your notes organized. Title and date your notes and keep them in chronological order in a binder.

Take notes in your textbook. Write summaries, questions, and ideas in the margins of your text. When you read with a pen at the ready, you interact with the text more and stay focused.

> **Effective notes identify the main** ideas of a lecture or text, identify pertinent supporting details, are organized and arranged in a way that enhances your understanding of the material, and make studying for the test much easier!
>
> *GOOD TO KNOW*

Create a formula and definitions sheet or note cards. This helps you memorize the formulas and definitions in two ways: 1) through the practice and repetition of writing them out, and 2) by writing a handy study sheet you can refer to throughout the semester.

Go light on the highlighter. The problem with highlighting is that it doesn't provide any other information. When you write in the margins of the book you can record your responses and ideas. When you highlight, you simply record lime green color.

You'll probably have a few months of trial and error with note taking before you hit on a system that fits your learning style. Before you know it, though, you'll have your own series of abbreviations and an enviable stock of notes to draw on as you prepare for finals.

The Hard-to-Follow Instructor

Don't give up! If you feel lost after a particularly difficult to understand lecture, **compare notes with classmates, use a recording device** (with permission, of course), **meet with your instructor** to review materials and ask questions, and **ask questions** during the lecture.

Studying

In a way, all the sections that came before this were also about studying. When you take good notes, you are studying. When you actively participate in class, you are studying. When you use the memorization methods discussed in Chapter 8, you are studying.

A narrow view of studying is that it's just for the days before the test. Not so. If you are attentive in each class period and review your notes regularly, you should theoretically get the best sleep of the semester during finals week.

The goal of studying is to own your knowledge–to remember and understand what you've learned—and, of course, to demonstrate that mastery on exams. Here's how:

Create a study plan. As a first-year college student you might have more free time than ever before—so it's especially important to learn how to provide structure for that time. Look at your weekly calendar and determine when you'll review notes for each class (we recommend doing so later the same day of the class), when you'll practice skills, when you'll work on assignments, etc. If you break down the work into smaller chunks of time–say, 1 to 2 hours—you'll stay more focused and you'll learn more than if you try to do everything in marathon study sessions. Pace yourself!

Study frequently. Review your notes and readings on a regular basis.

Know what you don't know. After you've reviewed your day's (or week's) notes, identify any holes in your knowledge and figure out who can help you with those missing pieces. You might ask your instructor, a study buddy, or a tutor in the department.

Quiz yourself. Use flashcards, double-sided notes, and other means to test your understanding and memory.

Teach someone. If you can explain the material to someone else, you've mastered it.

Collaborate. Study partners and groups are an excellent way to further understanding of material. They can teach you, you can teach them, and together you can figure out ways to remember ideas.

Commit. Effective studying requires concentration and time. Determine your purpose for wanting to do well, then commit to yourself.

Before you get too far into your first year, figure out which study conditions work best for you through a combination of trial and error and self-reflection. Be honest with yourself as you answer the questions on the next page. You might prefer to study in a bustling café filled with attractive people and pastries, but is that the optimum place to work?

Once you've filled out the Personal Study Conditions Inventory, we recommend you keep it handy. You'll have plenty of opportunities to get distracted in college and this inventory might remind you of your personal optimum study conditions.

Academic Support Resources

A hallmark of a master student is the ability to seek and obtain assistance. We recommend you get help before you even know you need it. Especially for your first term assignments, you should draw on available resources: do your math homework in the math lab, ask for feedback on your essays from the writing center staff, and get advice on preparing presentations from the staff of the speaking lab. Doing so can only help you—and it might prevent problems.

Potential resources include

- your instructor
- teaching assistants
- your advisor
- academic support services
- math, writing, or speaking labs
- Tutoring Center
- Computing Center
- Supplementary Instruction (SI) groups (study groups led by trained educators)
- online tutoring, labs, and writing resources

Don't fret if your writing skills are a little rusty or if your study habits have been lax in the past. A successful student always seeks improvement, never a perfection that does not exist. Being your own best teacher means challenging yourself, trying new approaches, and sometimes imposing discipline. The skills we discuss in this chapter are vital and well worth the effort it takes to master them.

Personal Study Conditions Inventory

Time

What times of day (or night) do I have the most energy?

When am I most focused?

When do I have the least energy?

When am I least focused?

Place

Where am I likely to maintain focus?

Where am I likely to be most productive?

Where am I likely to be inspired and motivated?

Where am I likely to be distracted and interrupted?

Mode

Do I study best with total quiet or some noise?

Do I study best in solitude or around people?

Do I stay more focused when I have a deadline?

Visit **www.LifeDuringCollege.com**
for more resources and exercises.

Communication, Note Taking & Study Skills **Exercises**

1. Try a new routine: If you usually study in your apartment, try studying in the library. If you usually study in the evening, try doing it in the afternoon. Note the pros and cons of each studying situation.

2. Create a 5-minute individual or group presentation on a topic related to this course. Ideas might include Study Habits, Places to Study, and the Most Valuable Resources on Campus. After your presentation, write a one-page reflection on the presentation's strengths and weaknesses.

3. Reflect on your participation skills: What are your strengths in this area? What are your weaknesses? Give yourself three specific challenges related to participation. How will you assess if you've been successful in meeting these challenges?

4. Try two of the four note-taking formats in one of your other classes this week. Write a reflection (outline form is OK) on which format you think was most effective and why.

Visit **www.LifeDuringCollege.com**
for more resources and exercises.

Academic Integrity

CHAPTER 10

Honor, Courage, and Commitment.

Honor, Respect, and Devotion to Duty.

Loyalty, Duty, Respect, Selfless Service, Honor, Integrity, and Personal Courage.

Integrity first, Service before self, and Excellence in all we do.

For veterans, core values suggest that you belong to something larger than yourself. Rooted in military tradition, these values create the high standards that guide both professional and personal conduct. It is important to reflect on your core values because during your college experience you may find yourself tempted to bend the rules. Cheating is tempting, easy, and costly. It's also on the rise, perhaps because certain websites and networks of students portray academic dishonesty as an inevitable part of college life or as a strategic tool to get ahead. Keep in mind that the consequences are many and may range from zero credit in a course to expulsion from school. Of course there are other unquantifiable consequences, such as an uneasy conscience and the feeling that you failed to honor your full potential.

In this chapter we will

- define academic integrity and academic dishonesty
- discuss the pressures or attitudes that encourage academic dishonesty and how to handle them
- outline some of the possible consequences of academic misconduct

What is Academic Integrity?

The core value of higher education is academic integrity. The Center for Academic Integrity, a consortium of institutions based at Clemson University, defines academic integrity as "a commitment, even in the face of adversity, to five fundamental values: honesty, trust, fairness, respect, and responsibility."

Students need to trust professors to teach and evaluate honorably and fairly, and professors need to trust their students to behave and act honorably and responsibly. A college without such standards would have no purpose: The interactions between students and professors would be pointless and a degree from such an institution would be meaningless.

Administrators, instructors, and students all have a responsibility for promoting and supporting academic integrity.

What is Academic Dishonesty?

Academic dishonesty encompasses a range of misdeeds, most of which involve taking credit for work, words, or knowledge that is not yours. Cheating includes:

- Turning in an assignment completed by someone else

- Obtaining an exam or exam questions before your exam time

- Giving or receiving answers on an exam (during or before the exam itself)

- Unauthorized storing of information in any form that may assist you on an exam

- Arranging to have someone take an exam on your behalf

- Aiding another person in an unauthorized manner (e.g., taking an exam on that student's behalf, writing a paper or sections of a paper on the student's behalf, etc.)

- Using unauthorized notes, study aids, or technology

- Collaborating without prior approval (e.g., completing an assignment with another student in class)

- Fabricating data, results, or sources

- Submitting work done for one instructor to another instructor (e.g., turning in the same essay to two different instructors)

- Falsifying records (e.g., forging a signature on a prerequisite form, breaking into the computer system to change a grade)

- Robbing other students of resources (e.g., tearing pages out of an academic journal in the library, hiding a book in the stacks of the library)

- Plagiarizing a book, article, Web site, or other source

> **PLAGIARISM:**
>
> Copying someone's work and passing it off as if it's your original idea. Give credit to the source of each idea, paraphrase, summary, and direct quote in your work. If no author is listed on the source material, credit the organization, article title, or website.
>
> *Good To Know*

While all of the examples listed above would be considered academically dishonest behavior at any school, it's a good idea to read over your school's honor code and/or academic honesty guidelines for more specific examples and information.

Plagiarism

Let's go into detail on this one, as it's the source of confusion for some students. **Plagiarism is copying someone's work and pretending you wrote it** (definition from www.justice.gov). **If you paraphrase, summarize, or directly quote another work you must cite your source! Not citing a source is the same thing as claiming the ideas and words are original to you; thus, it's plagiarism.** A recent *New York Times* article on plagiarism in the digital age explored how some students consider web content free, open, and therefore something one can use without giving credit. That is a dangerous presumption: Whether the source material has one author or a gazillion authors with none listed (e.g., Wikipedia), it needs to be cited.

When Do You Cite?

Generally, you want to cite when the following rules apply:

- You state something that could be challenged
- You state a fact or make a claim that is not common knowledge
- You quote somebody
- You paraphrase information from a source
- You reference data

Why do Students Cheat?

Students decide to cheat for a variety of reasons. The most common reasons are feeling insufficiently prepared, overloaded, or overwhelmed by personal issues. Other reasons include:

Environment. If the people around you consider cheating acceptable behavior, it can be easy to slip into the same mindset.

Poor pacing or preparation. Students who get behind sometimes consider cheating a means to an end. They see it as a lifesaver that will help avert an oncoming disaster. Other students feel underprepared and lack confidence in their own abilities, so they cover up their weaknesses by taking other people's work.

Pressure. Some students put enormous pressure on themselves to be successful, then feel they have to cheat in order to live up to their performance standards. Other students have pressure from parents or within their program to meet a certain grade point average.

Inability to say 'No.' Some students find it difficult to say no to friends who ask them to help cheat. They would rather avoid the awkwardness of denying a friend a favor and risk damaging their own academic credibility.

Collaboration or Cheating?

GOOD TO KNOW

In some circumstances, collaboration is valued, promoted, and even required. In other cases, collaboration is cheating. Check with your instructor to make sure you have his or her permission before you collaborate with another student or students.

How to Maintain Your Academic Integrity

The key to maintaining your credibility and academic honesty is to be vigilant. Scrutinize your own actions. Avoid justifications, such as "This professor is too hard anyway" or "I knew the material, I just didn't have the busywork part of it done" or "The deadline is unreasonable" or "Just this once."

Always ask yourself, "Will I be proud when I look back on this?" and "Would I do this if my professor were right here?"

Pace yourself to avoid a crisis situation where cheating seems like a good alternative. If you do procrastinate—and many of us do—turn in your own original work, even if it's poor. You can also try discussing the situation with your instructor to see if he or she would be amenable to accepting late work.

> *If you don't quit, and don't cheat, and don't run home when trouble arrives, you can only win.*
>
> **Shelley Long, American actress**

Get help when you don't understand a concept or just can't seem to master a skill. The tutoring center, the writing center, and your academic advisor should be able to help you or point you to the resources you need.

Be part of the solution. Hold yourself and others to high standards, and do your part to uphold the values of your college. Sometimes this means having to have an awkward conversation with a friend who has asked you to cheat. Sometimes it means informing an instructor when you know that classmates are cheating.

Because academic integrity is so highly valued, you will find that in general instructors and tutors respond very positively to students' requests for support and guidance in this area.

When a Friend or Classmate Cheats

What should you do if you suspect or know that a friend or classmate is cheating? Situations you might encounter include being asked to share exam questions and answers with somebody who hasn't yet taken the exam, learning that a friend has hired an essay writing "service", and witnessing a classmate using unauthorized materials (such as a cell phone or notes) during an exam. There are so many potential hypothetical situations that it's impossible to give just one answer.

A student who senses a classmate peering at her desk during an exam might simply shift positions to better hide her answers. We know at least a couple of students who dealt with similar situations by pretending to mark incorrect answers correct. While that might be an extreme response, it does stem from strong feelings that students need to earn their grades, not steal them.

Here are some possible steps to take if you strongly suspect or know that a friend or classmate is cheating. Not all situations are equal, so use your judgment as well as any guidelines provided by your school.

Review your school's honor code or academic honesty policies to see if there are recommended or required procedures to follow.

Communicate directly to the student(s) who is contemplating cheating or who has already done so and express your concerns.

Inform the instructor privately. A face-to-face conversation is best, but email will do if you have no alternative.

Telling on a fellow student seems distasteful to most people. However, knowing about an incident of academic dishonesty and not doing something to prevent or reveal it makes you complicit. Deal with the situation honorably and you will be able to balance your loyalty to your classmate and your loyalty to your school.

Consequences of Academic Dishonesty

Cheating in college is a serious offense that could result in significant consequences. In some cases, the instructor alone may reprimand a student who is caught cheating. However, many colleges require instructors to report any form of cheating to the college's administration.

Students who are accused of cheating usually are provided the opportunity to defend themselves to the department head, college administration, or even a student court. If the student is found guilty, he or she could face a variety of punishments, including failing the course, being put on suspension, or even being expelled. In addition to these punishments, the student may experience added stress, embarrassment, and loss of credibility. Additionally, in most cases, if a student is found guilty of cheating, the incident will be documented in the student's school records, which may cause considerable difficulty if the student applies to another institution to pursue an advanced degree.

GOOD TO KNOW: Some colleges have revoked degrees after determining that students had cheated.

In some cases, degrees have been revoked well after the students have graduated. In one famous case, a physics professor at the University of Virginia was informed that many students in his introductory physics classes had cheated on their term papers. When he investigated the accusation, he found that 122 of his students from the previous five semesters had indeed plagiarized. As many as half of those students were expelled from the university and several students who had already graduated had their degrees revoked.

Exams

Ironically, many veterans joke that they enlisted in the military out of high school so that they wouldn't have to take another exam ever again. However, to their surprise, they found themselves taking tests throughout their careers. Exams are one measure to evaluate how well a person understands a certain amount of material. While some people might consider exams a nightmare designed to weed out the faint of heart, like BUDS or Ranger School, it's important to remember that they exist for good reason. Namely, to consolidate learning. Exams provide an incentive to learn. They also give you a purpose for synthesizing the information and ideas you've encountered in a unit or semester – if you didn't go through the steps of reviewing, studying, and testing you wouldn't know the course content as deeply. Exams also serve as important indicators of gaps in your knowledge; in this way, both you and your instructor learn from your performance on an exam.

This chapter will

- walk you through exam anxiety

- help prepare you for the days before the exam

- offer unique strategies for taking various types of exams

- provide the hows and whys of reviewing a graded exam

Consider This ...

Important for veterans

What some veterans perceive as test anxiety may actually be a medical condition such as depression, traumatic brain injury, or post-traumatic stress. Instead of attempting to diagnose the condition by yourself, it is important to seek professional guidance through Disability Support Services and the Counseling Center.

Dealing with Test Anxiety

Almost everybody gets the pre-test jitters. In fact, some of that nervousness may help bolster performance. Some students, however, experience intense anxiety. According to Greenberger and Padesky, clinical psychologists and authors of *Mind Over Mood*, "Anxiety can be reduced either by decreasing your perception of danger or increasing your confidence in the ability to cope with threat." When we apply that statement to test taking, we need to ask, "What is the perception of danger?" and "How does one increase confidence in one's ability to cope?"

We'll let you answer the first question for yourself. Here are some tips for increasing confidence in your abilities:

Give yourself sufficient time to prepare for the exam.

Imagine the test as one step in a process (after all, it is!). Notice how successfully you complete each step (the steps might include attending class, taking notes, creating a study guide, completing practice quizzes, and taking the test).

Schedule an appointment with your instructor at least one week prior to the exam if you have questions about any material that confuses you.

Participate in a study group or prepare with another student.

Visualize yourself succeeding on the exam.

Avoid studying with other students who seem intensely anxious.

Check with your college's counseling center. Many offer workshops and guidance for preparing for exams and addressing test anxiety.

You can't avoid exams in college, so you'll have many opportunities to face your fears and build up your confidence. If you have such bad test anxiety that you *do* avoid exams you should make an appointment with your academic advisor and/or a counselor to discuss how your fear is impacting your studies.

Test Anxiety Worksheet

My specific fears related to test taking:

Steps I can take to increase my confidence:

Visit **www.LIfeDuringCollege.com**
to download a copy of this form.

Preparing for an Exam

The biggest mistake students tend to make before an exam is to disrupt their normal schedules. Preparing for an exam in such a way interferes with familiar sleeping, eating, and other habits and makes it difficult to concentrate on the task at hand. Here are some ways to make the most of the night before and the day of an exam:

Maintain a regular diet and sleep schedule. Staying up late and snacking on unhealthy foods can not only diminish your performance on the exam, but also add unneeded stress.

Give yourself sufficient time to gather necessary materials. Doing so will ensure that you have everything you need when you get to the exam and you won't be madly scrambling to get out of your apartment.

Do what you need to do to be alert, whether that's taking a shower, having a real breakfast, or going out for a run.

If allowed, bring a small snack and/or drink into the exam room so that you can maintain energy throughout the test.

Glance through your study materials on the morning of the exam to refresh your memory.

Cramming

No one will recommend cramming for an exam, but if you do find yourself in such a situation, here's the right way to cram:

Maintain a positive attitude. If you attended the class and completed your assignments, you should do fine on the exam. Sure, you could do better with more time to study, but you'll do the best you can do with the limited time you have left.

Make efficient use of the time you do have. Focus on the concepts and ideas with which you are unfamiliar, rather than reviewing materials you already know well.

Take frequent, short breaks about once an hour to stretch and walk around a little. This will keep you active, alert, and awake.

Study in a location that encourages concentration, such as a desk or table. Avoid studying on your bed, sofa, or anywhere that will be too comfortable and distracting.

Avoid stimulants like coffee, soda, or energy drinks that might keep you alert for a time, but leave you in an extremely drowsy or agitated state.

Eat healthy foods while you are studying and immediately prior to the exam.

Try to get sufficient rest so that you can think clearly during the exam.

Strategies for Taking an Exam

Having a game plan to follow on exam day will make the experience less stressful. The following are strategies that should help you through the examination process.

Arrive early. Have your materials ready and find a comfortable seat. In fact, sitting in your regular seat can help you recall information.

Relax and think positively: *I can do this. I know this stuff.*

Dress appropriately. This seems silly, but being too hot or too cold can easily distract you.

Preview the exam. When you receive your exam, take a few minutes to look it over. Make sure you check each page, front and back, so you don't miss a section. This will allow you to determine the amount of time you should spend on each part.

Read the instructions carefully. It takes time to do, but it's critical. There have been countless points lost by not following directions.

Start with what you know. Some exam questions must be approached in sequence. However, with some exams you can skip around and answer the questions you know first. There are advantages to doing this: it builds confidence, maximizes the number of points you'll earn, and allows you more time later in the test to tackle the really tough questions. Also, answering questions you know immediately might help jog your memory for those that are more difficult.

Write legibly. Instructors can't grade what they can't read. If your instructor has to squint and puzzle through big chunks of your writing, she or he will give up and only give you points for those parts he or she can read. Take the time to write clearly.

Show your work. Leave a record of your thought process so your instructor can see how you arrived at your answer. Sometimes you'll get partial credit for taking the correct steps even if you ended with a wrong answer.

Concentrate. Easier said than done, but try to zero in on your exam, not on the sniffles and coughing coming from your classmates.

Don't panic if you don't know the answer to a question. Skip that question and come back to it after you've answered the ones you know. It's usually best to attempt an answer even if you're pretty sure it will be wrong. You might get partial credit if you can demonstrate some knowledge related to the question.

Learn from the exam as you take it. On many exams, questions build on one another or provide clues for other questions' answers.

Take time at the end of the exam. If possible, give yourself a chance to review your test after you complete it.

Hand in your test on time. Students have received a score of zero for not turning in a test on time. Don't take a risk.

In this section we'll discuss ways of approaching the most common types of exams you'll encounter: essay, true/false, multiple choice, open book/open note, take-home, and oral exams.

Essay Exams

- Read all questions thoroughly before you begin. Answer questions you feel most comfortable with first.

- Make a quick outline of key points and ideas before you begin writing. This will help prevent the "Oh no! I'm writing my conclusion and I finally know what I want to say!" experience.

- Get to the point. Make your focus clear from the outset of your essay and maintain that focus throughout the body paragraphs.

- Leave extra space between paragraphs and in the margins of your answer, in case you need to add additional information later. This isn't always possible, as some essay tests have a page limit and you won't be able to afford any blank space.

- Use specific, relevant details to support your point and prove your understanding of the material. Cite course materials if necessary.

- Use transition words and phrases to signal a shift in ideas. (e.g., "Not only…, but also…" or "Another example is…") These transitions will make your essay smooth and easy to read.

- Write legibly. Your instructor can't grade what he or she can't read.

True/False Exams

- If possible, skim over all the statements before you begin. Answer the statements you know first then return to those you don't know.

- Pay attention to wording. Read the statements very carefully: if any part of the statement is false, you need to mark "False." Some wording, such as the use of double negatives, can be very confusing.

- Watch out for key words or qualifiers such as "all," "most," "sometimes," "never," or "rarely." Although the answer to a statement may appear to be true at first, the addition of one of these key words can change the meaning of the statement and make it false.

Multiple-Choice Exams

- If possible, skim over all the questions before starting the exam and answer those you know the answers to first.

- Anticipate the answer as you read the question, then find the available choice that best matches your answer.

- If you are unsure of the answer to a question, read over all the answers provided. Use the process of elimination to narrow down your choices.

- If there is no penalty for incorrect answers, guess on those questions you don't know. If there is a penalty, it may not be worth it to guess.

Open Book/Open Note Exams

These can be the most difficult tests to take, perhaps because students underestimate them. Here are some tips to help you succeed on this type of exam:

WATCH OUT! GOOD TO KNOW
Open book exams are often more difficult than other types of exams.

- Study for open book/open note exams just as you would for a closed book one. Many students under prepare because they know they'll have access to their materials.

- Organize your notes and mark your textbook before the exam so you don't spend precious time searching for information.

- Read all the questions first, then answer the ones you know immediately. You may want to confirm you know the answer by checking in your materials, but it's not always necessary.

- Use your materials. Your instructor expects more detail and diligence than he or she would of a closed book test. Use direct quotes if appropriate, cite sources whenever possible, and include specific details if you have them and they're relevant to your answers.

Take-Home Exams

As with open book/open note exams, many students fail to prepare sufficiently for take-home exams. Here's how to succeed on them:

Instructors often have higher expectations for take-home exams than in-class exams. TIP

- Organize all study materials, such as notes, reading, and homework assignments.

- Review the exam thoroughly before you leave the classroom. If you have any questions, ask the instructor. Also, ask if and how the instructor can be contacted if you have additional questions later.

- Do thorough work. Instructors have higher standards for take-home tests than for in-class ones.

- Stay focused. It may be tempting with all of the time you have for the assignment to write more or do additional, unnecessary work. Develop thorough responses to the question(s), but don't waste your time—or your instructor's—with unrelated information.

- Use your materials. Your instructor expects more detail and diligence than he or she would of a closed book test. Use direct quotes if appropriate, cite sources whenever possible, and include specific details if you have them and they're relevant to your answers.

Oral Exams

These tests are more common during graduate school, but you might encounter an oral exam as an undergraduate.

- Prepare materials for the exam just as you would for an essay or other test. Your oral exam answers should have key points and support for those points.

- Make sure you understand the requirements and expectations.

- Practice with another student, if possible.

- Time yourself when you practice if your oral exam will be timed.

- If your instructor allows a few moments to gather your thoughts before you launch into an answer, use that time.

- Be concise and clear with your response. Use signal words to help your listener follow your ideas. ("*Another* piece of evidence that supports my point is…" or "My *second* rationale is…") Avoid rambling.

Check it Twice!

Before you turn in your exam, double check it to make sure you've taken care of the details. Some common mistakes are easily avoidable. Follow these steps every time:

Make sure your name, student identification number, and other required information is included on your exam.

Double check the Scantron/bubble form (if applicable) to verify you've filled in the correct bubble for each question.

Review the exam and instructions a final time to ensure that you have fulfilled all the requirements.

Review Your Graded Exam

You probably won't post your graded exam on the refrigerator, but you definitely should review it. Why? One reason is to check for any mistakes in calculations your instructor or TA might have made. The other, more powerful, reason is to learn from the mistakes you made and the test itself.

The following tips will help you effectively review your exam:

Calculate your score to verify that the grader computed it correctly.

Review the exam for answers that were marked wrong but you still think are correct. Rework the answers, this time with all the resources available to you. If you cannot arrive at the correct answer on your own, ask for assistance from the tutoring center or your instructor.

Analyze the test itself: Where do the questions originate? Lectures? Textbook? Assignments? This will make it easier for you to focus your studying for the next exam for that instructor.

Correct each of the incorrect and partially correct answers to better understand why they were wrong or what they were missing. Sometimes instructors provide model answers to assist students with this process.

Schedule an appointment with your instructor to discuss any questions you may have and to ask for his or her advice on studying for future exams.

Exams are a necessary if not entirely pleasant part of the learning process. Stay focused on your ultimate goal—learning—and you'll be able to diffuse some of the stress exams cause. Approach each class hour and study session with a desire to learn, and tests will become just another step in the process.

Exams **Exercises**

1. What is your standard method for studying for exams? Rate its effectiveness on a scale from 1 to 10, where 1 is least effective and 10 is most effective. Explain your rating.

2. What tips from this chapter are you most likely to try? Why?

3. What style of exam (essay, true/false, multiple-choice, etc.) do you find most difficult? Why?

4. Describe an excellent test you've taken: one that challenged you, truly assessed your knowledge, and taught you something valuable. Discuss with a partner.

5. Read the following statement, then discuss the following questions with a partner or group:

   Students tend to focus too much on the grade associated with an exam and not enough on the value of learning in preparation for it.

   Do you think this statement is true?

   What can instructors and institutions do to help students focus more on the value of learning?

   What can students do to help themselves focus more on the value of learning?

Visit **www.LifeDuringCollege.com**
for more resources and exercises.

Grades

CHAPTER 12

Good grades open doors. Graduate school admissions officers consider overall grade point average (GPA) as well as grades in specific course work. So, too, do future employers. In fact, according to the National Association of Colleges and Employers' Job Outlook 2013 survey, "more than 78 percent [of employers] say that they will screen candidates by GPA."

The job market plays a role here: When employers have an abundance of applicants, standards go up. If an employer has a GPA cutoff, it will likely be higher in years of high unemployment.

Good grades aren't the only way to advance. Internship experience and commitment to extracurricular activities are also highly valued. However, it's worth noting how important grades are so that you can take steps now to do well in your classes—and to maintain a solid GPA throughout your college years.

> **3.0** — *GOOD TO KNOW*
>
> **Most of the employers who have a GPA cutoff—in other words, who won't consider applicants with less than a certain GPA—report that 3.0 is the magic number. Other criteria include the applicant's college, major, and experience.**
>
> Source:
> NACE Job Outlook 2013 Survey

This chapter will

- provide an overview of grading systems

- outline alternative grading options

- illustrate the value of earning good grades your first year

- recommend strategies to maintain good grades

Grading Systems

Instructors work hard to grade fairly and accurately, but the methods of grading vary widely and may cause confusion for students. Some instructors assess student performance based on one or two major written assignments; others don't grade written work but calculate students' grades based on a test or two per semester. Some instructors grade participation, some offer extra credit assignments, some drop the lowest exam grade. The course syllabus should explain how students are assessed.

Despite the variation in methods and means of grading, there are only two major grading systems that you're likely to encounter:

Absolute Grading

This is the most common grading system. The instructor sets the point or percentage range for each letter grade at the beginning of the term. For example, a score of 90% or above is predetermined to be an A. Theoretically, with the absolute grading system, every student in class could get an A on a given test.

Relative Grading

Also known as "grading on a curve." This is a more competitive grading system, as each student's performance is evaluated against her peers. There are many ways to curve grades. Here's one example: Let's say the average score in the class is a 79%. If the instructor uses a standard deviation calculation to determine the cutoffs for each grade, an 89-100% is an A, 85-88% is a B, 72-84% is a C, 60-71% is a D, and 59% or below is a failing grade.

Make sure you understand within the first week of school the processes and systems that each of your instructors use. If the grading criteria are unclear, ask your instructor to clarify.

Grading Options

There are alternatives to receiving a letter grade for a class.

Pass/Fail

Many colleges allow some variation of the Pass/Fail option, though it's usually available only for non-required courses or electives. This is a great alternative for students interested in taking a certain class who want to limit the stress of working for a grade. Some schools encourage students to pursue curiosity and passion by taking interesting classes outside of their department, using the Pass/Fail option. For example, a History major fascinated by Physics might elect to take a Physics class Pass/Fail. Usually, your instructor will not know you are taking the course as a Pass/Fail. He or she will submit your grade to the registrar, who will convert it to a P or F on your transcript.

Incomplete

The incomplete is a good option for students who have experienced a major event or illness that has interfered with their ability to complete coursework. A student who is interested in pursuing this alternative needs to discuss it with his or her instructor and get permission. Usually, the student and instructor will then agree on a completion date that is some time after the actual end of the course. An "Incomplete" will appear on the student's transcript until the completion date. The student needs to submit all work and take all exams by that completion date in order to earn a letter grade for the course. A missed deadline may result in an F.

Withdrawal

There is a window of time after the term begins when a student can add or drop a course without the change affecting his or her transcript. This allows students to attend classes for the first few meetings and make an informed decision to stay in a class, switch to another class, or drop the class altogether. If a student withdraws after a certain date, however, a W will appear on his or her transcript.

Challenging Your Grade

Even college instructors make mistakes. You may find that an exam or assignment has been graded incorrectly. You may think that a question was worded awkwardly, which led you to answer it incorrectly. Or you may feel an instructor has treated you and your work unfairly. If any of these situations occur,

Gather the information you need to make your case. Refer to class notes, textbooks, previous assignments, and tests.

Make an appointment to discuss your concerns with your instructor.

Avoid defensiveness and anger. Listen to your instructor's reasoning carefully so you fully understand the situation.

If you are still not satisfied after meeting with your instructor, make an appointment to discuss your concerns with your academic advisor and ask for her or his advice.

If you are still not satisfied, you can petition to have the grade changed through the department committee that oversees the course.

The Value of Starting Strong

It's a lot easier to start off with a good grade point average than to dig out of a hole later. If you start strong and keep the momentum going, you won't have to worry so much about your grade slipping when you're in the really challenging classes your last two years of college. Here's an illustration that tracks the progress of two hypothetical students, Alex and Pat.

As you can see, Alex did poorly the first term and well the second term. However, Alex has a long way to go to raise his cumulative GPA and his classes will only get more difficult.

First Term	Alex	Pat
Chemistry *(4 credit hours)*	C	A
Anthropology *(3 credit hours)*	B	A
Creative Writing *(4 credit hours)*	C	A
Calculus *(4 credit hours)*	B	A
Grade Point Average	2.47	4.0

Second Term	Alex	Pat
Chemistry II *(4 credit hours)*	B	B
Art History *(3 credit hours)*	A	B
Biology *(4 credit hours)*	A	B
Calculus II *(4 credit hours)*	A	A
Grade Point Average	3.73	3.27

Cumulative Grade Point Average	3.10	3.63

Starting college with good grades is like an insurance policy: it protects you from potential GPA damage if you get a lower grade later in your college career.

Strategies for Maintaining Good Grades

Well, you could sign up for the easiest courses and take the bare minimum number of credits necessary to maintain enrollment and/or financial aid. It wouldn't be very rewarding, though. Here's how to challenge yourself, get an excellent education, *and* maintain good grades:

DO:

Focus on learning. Attend class, study, and complete course work. When you master the material, the grades will show it.

Balance your course load. Take a reasonable number of classes, and balance very challenging classes with not-so-difficult ones.

Make sure you understand the objectives of the course and how you'll be evaluated.

Connect with your instructors. Get comfortable with asking questions and asking for assistance. Discuss any concerns you have with your instructor. If you feel an error has been made, bring it to your instructor's attention.

DON'T:

Lose focus as you enjoy your college freedom. First-year grades do matter and they can be hard to make up for later.

Overload yourself with too many challenging classes in the same term.

Give up. Any improvement you make in your grades—either in a specific course during a term or in your overall grade point average—will help and is worth the effort.

Get defensive or angry if you disagree with a grade you have received. Become familiar with how your college handles these kinds of situations and participate in the process.

Grades **Exercises**

1. Review the syllabi of the classes you're enrolled in this term. What are the grading procedures of each instructor?

2. Research alternative grading options available at your college and the requirements for electing those alternatives.

Visit **www.LifeDuringCollege.com**
for more resources and exercises.

Keys to Success

CHAPTER 13

Intelligence, ambition, and hard work can carry you far, but true success depends on other factors that aren't so measurable. For instance, "Loose lips sink ships" is an old Navy saying about the importance of safeguarding sensitive information. However, many veterans also know this as a mantra for not getting caught up in rumors, gossip, and the other drama that sink morale or limit productivity. Whether deployed, underway, attending a drill weekend, or progressing toward your degree, your life in general and college experience in particular will be richer if you

- maintain a positive attitude
- develop high self-esteem and self-efficacy
- set goals and make plans for attaining them; understand that goals take time
- know how to contribute to and get the most out of teamwork
- explore and celebrate the diversity around you

And, coincidentally, this chapter will cover all those topics!

Attitude

What is credited with delaying aging and has (practically) its own section in the book store? That's right: A positive attitude. It's not measured on any report card, but it's one of the most important attributes a college student can possess. Your attitude towards your classes, living situation, peers, and yourself may be even more influential to your success and happiness than your skills, talents, and knowledge. And if you don't already tend to have a positive attitude, there's good news: You can learn to develop a habit of positive thinking. In this section, we'll

- define a positive attitude
- share how to create and maintain a positive attitude

What is a Positive Attitude?

It's difficult to pinpoint just what separates those with positive attitudes from those without, but there are some traits closely associated with positive attitudes:

Optimism - Positive people tend to have hope and to see the good in a situation.

Persistence - Positive people believe problems can be resolved and puzzles can be solved. Their hope leads them to persist.

Enthusiasm and energy - Positive people exhibit enthusiasm in day-to-day life.

Curiosity - Positive people are curious about the world and are driven by the desire to learn.

Creativity - Positive people are able to shift perspectives and consider problems and ideas from new angles.

Confidence - Positive people have high self-esteem and are confident in their abilities.

Resourcefulness - Positive people work to find a solution when they encounter a problem.

Vision - Positive people envision possibilities and see the best in things—and people.

Sense of purpose - Positive people believe they have a purpose in life and act on that assumption.

Strong relationships - Positive people cultivate good relationships with family, friends, and neighbors.

10 Steps to a Positive Attitude

Learning to create and maintain a positive attitude will help you enjoy college and get more out of it.

1. Give yourself a dose of perspective.

You got a bad grade on a test, you argued with your roommate, and your veterans benefits are delayed. It's difficult to be positive when things pile up like this. But putting things into perspective can keep you emotionally afloat. Try viewing your situation from another angle: What did you do right? What will you learn from the experience? How could it be worse? Is it as bad as being underway and separated from your family? Is it more challenging than being stationed at a remote outpost in Afghanistan? Chances are you have already endured challenging situations and walked away stronger. How can you grow from your current experience?

2. Be confident.

Believe in yourself and your abilities. For example, if you got a bad grade on a test, have confidence that you will work hard to figure out how to do better.

3. Surround yourself with positive people.
Seek out interesting, enthusiastic people. Reconsider relationships you have with people who thrive on negativity and bring you down.

4. Don't dwell.
Yes, you want to reflect on your actions, accomplishments, and mistakes. But use that self-reflection to move forward. Too much attention on the past can result in what one of our colleagues aptly calls "Analysis Paralysis."

5. Get busy.
It's hard to dwell on the negative when you are involved in activities you enjoy, like sports, clubs, or volunteering.

6. Plan.
Plan things you can look forward to and work toward.

7. Learn from mistakes.
We'll let Winston Churchill take this one: "All men make mistakes, but only wise men learn from their mistakes."

8. Be flexible.
There's only so much you can control, and some of the most interesting and inspiring moments will come when you haven't planned on them.

9. Communicate positively.
You've seen the signs: "See something? Say something!" OK, in one context it's an anti-terrorism slogan. But in another context it can be an affirming reminder to celebrate the positive. See something cool? Say it's cool. Compliment, thank, and congratulate people in your life.

10. Make a commitment and follow through.
Few things are as gratifying as reaching a goal you have worked hard to achieve. Set short-term and long-term goals, commit to them, and celebrate your accomplishments.

Maintain Your Positive Attitude
Positive thinking is a habit that needs to be cultivated and supported. Different people have different requirements for maintaining a positive outlook, but we can boil the specifics down to three general tips that might have echoes from Kindergarten:

Be nice to yourself. Everything is going to look pretty dim pretty fast if you are exhausted, starving, and stressed out. Treat yourself well: eat healthily, get enough sleep, and pace yourself.

Be nice to others. Show interest in others by listening, asking questions, and paying attention. Express gratitude and praise when it's appropriate. Help out a friend who's struggling.

Look for good. Attend each lecture or activity with an eye toward the positive. Look for at least one good thing about each class period or event.

Self-Esteem and Self-Efficacy

In this section we'll talk about two factors critical to success and happiness: self-esteem and self-efficacy. Don't worry, we won't suggest you paste up sticky-notes with happy messages to yourself all over your apartment. If you want to do that, great, but our mission here is simply to define self-esteem and self-efficacy, discuss their importance in one's life in college and beyond, and provide tips for developing them.

Self-Esteem

Self-esteem is the pride and respect one has for oneself. If you hold someone in high esteem, you value and respect them. If you hold *yourself* in high esteem, you value and respect yourself. High self-esteem is not cockiness; in fact, most people with high self-esteem do not brag or flaunt their stuff because they don't rely on extrinsic validation. People with high self-esteem tend to value and respect others.

Self-esteem is reflected in the way you

- talk to yourself
- think about yourself and others
- meet a challenge
- respond to criticism
- face adversity

The inner monologue reveals how a person sees him or herself. A person who dwells on his or her weaknesses and failures—and, by contrast, everyone else's strengths and successes—will tell him or herself disrespectful "truths":

Low Self-Esteem Statements	High Self-Esteem Statements
Everyone else is better at this than I am.	*I can do this!*
I'm worthless.	*I accept and like myself.*
I messed up again! That's just like me.	*I made a mistake.*

By making yourself aware of your own inner monologue, you can adjust it to be kinder, more forgiving, and more celebratory.

Self-esteem also affects how you respond to criticism and setbacks. Someone with low self-esteem will perceive criticism as a direct attack or proof that his low opinion of himself is well-founded. If he experiences a setback, he will give up. By contrast, a person with high self-esteem will be much more persistent and less likely to see criticism as a personal affront.

Your self-esteem will affect your academic life, so it's a good idea to reflect on your perceptions of yourself and to make sure they will have a positive influence.

> *It is of practical value to learn to like yourself. Since you must spend so much time with yourself you might as well get some satisfaction out of the relationship.*
>
> **Norman Vincent Peale, American author**

The National Association for Self-Esteem has a tool on its website that allows visitors to answer a series of questions and rate their self-esteem. **www.self-esteem-nase.org**

GOOD TO KNOW

The Self-Esteem Workout

Here are some exercises you can do on a regular basis to bolster your self-esteem:

Don't compare. Value yourself, value others, and don't waste time measuring the differences.

Don't dwell. Move on from past mistakes and embarrassments. If you find yourself dwelling on something, get busy or get help.

Be accountable. Taking responsibility for your own actions will help you respect yourself more.

Develop diverse interests. Imagine a three-year-old at a playground. There's no "I won't go on the slide, I'm not really good at slides, I'll just stick to sitting in these wood chips!" Very young kids just do whatever seems interesting to them; they don't talk themselves out of new experiences. Now imagine yourself 30 years from now: What activity or interest will you be proud of yourself for trying? Will you care if you weren't perfect at it?

Compliment others. Recognizing others for their successes is great practice for recognizing your own.

Take risks. When you take a risk and succeed you've just amped up your willingness to take another, bigger risk. When you take a risk and you fail you can congratulate yourself for trying.

Give yourself credit—and rewards. Remind yourself of your successes, talents, and good qualities.

Be grateful. Divert negative thoughts away by reflecting on the things for which you are grateful.

Take care of yourself. If you value yourself, you value your health. When you feel healthy, you're more likely to feel good about your overall well-being.

> *So why do I talk about the benefits of failure? Simply because failure meant a stripping away of the inessential. I stopped pretending to myself that I was anything other than what I was, and began to direct all my energy into finishing the only work that mattered to me.*
>
> JK Rowling, British author,
> Harvard Commencement Address, June 2008

Self-Efficacy

Albert Bandura, the influential Stanford psychologist, defines **perceived self-efficacy** as "people's beliefs about their capabilities to produce designated levels of performance that exercise influence over events that affect their lives. Self-efficacy beliefs determine how people feel, think, motivate themselves and behave." A person with high perceived self-efficacy believes she or he is very capable of performing well and can influence her or his own life.

What is your perceived self-efficacy? Do you believe you are capable? Do you believe you have influence over your life?

It depends, right? Most of us, if challenged to grow three feet taller or to become invisible or to be the next NBA superstar by Wednesday, would have low self-efficacy. We would doubt our capabilities to accomplish those goals because they are impossible or next to impossible. We would feel frustrated or apathetic, think "I can't. No way!" We would be completely unmotivated and behave accordingly.

If, on the other hand, we were challenged to learn to snowboard, or paint with watercolors, or make a birdhouse, most of us would have significantly higher perceived self-efficacy. Some students enter college with a strong sense of their capabilities, and others need to develop theirs. In order to understand your own perception of self-efficacy, consider the influences on it:

Success and failure. If you try something and succeed, you'll be more likely to think you can do it again or to do the next step in the process. Bandura terms these "mastery experiences." Think about your first time at bat in a baseball game or the first time you completed a set of fractions: how did those mastery experiences influence your next attempt? Failure can influence a person as well. When you have a strong sense of efficacy, though, you tend to see failure as temporary and it challenges you to redouble your efforts. The author J.K. Rowling, for example, received multiple rejections before a publishing house took a chance on her book, *Harry Potter and the Sorcerer's Stone*. Her persistence paid off, to say the least.

Social models. When we see people around us accomplish something it shows us that it's possible and that we can do it, too. On the other hand, if there are no models we might think something is out of reach or impossible.

Social persuasion. Other people around us give us messages about our abilities, for better and for worse. If you believe these other people they can be very influential. Think about the teacher who believed in you when you didn't. (Or the teacher who didn't believe in you.) Parents, teachers, and peers have a big impact on us—that can last well beyond our time with them.

Emotional states. Think about how difficult some tasks seem when you're overtired, or how little energy you may feel when you're sad. Our state of being influences how we interpret our performance and our perception of our own efficacy.

The above information was adapted from Albert Bandura's work. See Sources section for more information.

Developing Self-Efficacy

Once you understand the influences on your perception of self-efficacy, possibilities open up for how to develop it. Here are some:

Set yourself up for success. Give yourself tasks where you can be successful. Break up big projects into little chunks and note your ability to tackle them.

Consider failures opportunities. A failure isn't a stop sign; it's a detour.

Choose your social models. Hang out with friends who inspire you and believe in you and do the same for them. Connect with instructors you admire and respect.

Recognize your emotional state. If you do poorly on a test, recognize the physiological and emotional factors that influenced your performance. Were you exhausted? Overly anxious? Depressed? Don't see your poor test score as indicative of you in general but of your performance on a given day in certain circumstances.

Goal Setting

A successful college student sets goals and makes specific plans for achieving them. This section will show you how to do just that, by discussing

- how to set goals
- how to establish meaningful goals
- how to stay motivated

Five Steps to Setting Goals

Here's a process for setting goals that ensures you attain them:

1. Establish a realistic goal

First, ask yourself what you want to accomplish. Be specific. For example, if you want to improve your grades, clarify what grade you'd like to earn in each class.

2. Create an action plan

There is never just one way to accomplish a goal, but there is some way. If you want to be successful, be as specific as possible when you create your plan. If your goal is to run a marathon eight months from now, for example, your action plan should include how many miles per week you need to run, what kind of adjustments you will need to make to your diet, and what time of day will be best for your training.

3. Divide your goal into smaller achievements

Learn Mandarin Chinese! Save $10,000! Get a 4.0! Goals can be daunting sometimes. Make it less intimidating—and more achievable—by breaking it into smaller, more accessible goals. For example, if your goal is to learn a new language, you might break it into the following steps: register for an introductory class, join an evening conversation group, spend a term in a country where that language is spoken, etc.

4. Set a target date
You've seen the inspirational posters: A goal is a dream with a deadline. It's true. A person decides she'll get out of credit card debt. But when? Next month? In 40 years? What if she pays off the plastic in April and runs it up again in June? How will she know if she's achieved the goal satisfactorily? Be specific with your timeline so you can stay motivated.

5. Identify your motivators
Speaking of motivation, what's yours? The rest of these tips focus on the How, but this one is about the Why. Why do you want to get in shape? To look good? To improve your health? To perform better in your favorite sport? When you identify *why* you want to do something you will be better able to stay on track.

Meaningful Goals

Setting impossible goals is a sure way to frustrate yourself; setting trivial ones won't do much for you either. The key is to develop realistic, meaningful goals. Here's how:

Let me tell you the secret that has led me to my goal. My strength lies solely in my tenacity.

Louis Pasteur

Think short-term and long-term. Some goals are accomplished in one week; others take years. Establish both kinds for yourself so you get the satisfaction of achievement along the way to your bigger goals.

Make sure they're your goals. Your mom might want you to pursue a career in medicine, your classmates might expect you to go into law, but if your heart tells you to become a physical therapist—well, others' plans for you don't matter. Similarly, if everyone else is set on getting a high-paying job right after college and you don't hear that particular siren's call, decide what *you* want to do.

Prioritize. Sometimes goals compete for time and attention. You may want to earn a 3.6 this semester, learn to play banjo, and meet new friends. Which is most important? Which one needs to be addressed right away and which one can wait? The answers will depend on you.

Challenge yourself. Sure, you want realistic, achievable goals, but they should also stretch you. If your goals are too easy to achieve, you might become bored or not enjoy the satisfaction of accomplishing them.

Be flexible. Things change and you may need to adjust a goal or replace it with another one, or you might need to alter the action plan and find a new way to achieve the goal.

Staying Motivated

Your motivation level is probably the most important factor in determining your success. Here are strategies to get and stay motivated:

Build reminders into your life. It's surprisingly easy to lose sight of something that seemed ultra-important just hours or days before. Write down your goals and post them in a place you'll see regularly (screen savers and refrigerators were made for this type of thing!).

Focus on results. Keep your desired end result in mind. Let's say your goal is to earn an A in Organic Chemistry. There will be moments throughout the term when you may want to skip a lecture or hang out with friends rather than study. If you begin to waver, pause to think about how it will feel to get that A, and how you will be able to use the knowledge you gain from this term to move on to the next level of science.

Share. You should share your goals with at least a couple of people. Knowing that others are aware of your goals and are rooting you on will help keep you enthusiastic and accountable.

Reward yourself. Recognize and celebrate your achievements.

Teamwork

So far this chapter has focused on the individual – personal attitudes, perceptions, and goals – but much of your college experience will be about the other people you encounter. And at least some of the college experience will involve working very closely with others in teams. But, you're in luck. As a veteran, this is not new territory for you.

Can we choose our groups? Can we pick our teams? Remember that first day in basic training or boot camp when everything was confusing and you could hardly march down to the chow hall in sync? When the drill sergeant barked, "left face!" the guy next to you turned right and from there it got worse. You've experienced the joys and horrors of initial military training, and from day one, you learned that the only way to survive was by working as a team. You've seen the meltdown of a dysfunctional platoon, when the bickering escalates and the rhythm slows. But, you have also seen the magical moments when everything is in step like a fine oiled machine that runs flawlessly.

Whatever your feelings about working on teams, you will probably have many opportunities to work through them in college.

In this section we'll

- explain what makes a good team member
- describe the qualities of a successful team
- recommend strategies for getting the most out of the team experience

What is a Team Player?

In most college classes, extracurricular clubs, and offices a team player is defined a bit differently:

Skillful - Every member of the team needs to bring some talent and skills to the group.

Cooperative - While leadership gets a lot of press, cooperation is even more important. A good team player pulls his or her weight, minimizes conflict, stays positive, and encourages others to do the same.

A good communicator - Failure to communicate well is one of the biggest sources of conflict in teams. Effective communication is very valuable.

Committed - A good team player lets her or his teammates know she or he is committed to the common cause and can be counted on.

Honest - Honesty is necessary to establishing trust between team members.

Responsible - Good team players share the credit, and don't blame others.

Successful Teams

You have a team made up of great members. Excellent! What's the next step? To be successful, teams must possess:

Purpose - The members must understand their mission.

Empowerment - A strong team feels empowered to work and create solutions, and well-supported by their leaders and resources.

Good communication - Members should listen, speak, and discuss frankly and respectfully.

Flexibility - A good team can adapt and adjust to changing circumstances and expectations.

Productivity - A team gets the job done efficiently and effectively.

Morale - A good team keeps morale high even in high-pressure situations.

Strategies for Getting the Most Out of Working With a Team

The following are ways you can ensure success for the team:

Create clear goals. Team members must understand their goals, believe those goals are worthwhile, know what they are expected to accomplish, and understand how they will work together to achieve those goals.

Aim for small victories. Focus on small, short-term successes to build the confidence necessary to achieve the overall goal.

Build mutual trust. Trust takes a long time to build and an instant to shatter. To build trust, team members must be approachable, respectful, objective, dependable, and willing to listen.

Ensure mutual accountability and a sense of common purpose. All members must feel accountable.

Secure the resources you need. If your team is dependent on resources from outside sources, make sure they're in place before you proceed.

Develop your skills. This is the time to strengthen areas of weakness. Problem solving, communication, negotiation, conflict resolution, and writing skills are all areas where most students can improve.

Diversity

Many people think of diversity only as it relates to ethnicity. Advertisements intended to portray an organization or its members as diverse will include images of people with a range of skin colors. But diversity encompasses much more than that and does not just pertain to visible characteristics. In fact, there are many aspects to diversity. Here are just some:

- Age
- Gender
- Ethnicity
- Cultural heritage
- Mental/physical abilities
- Mental/physical characteristics
- Sexual orientation
- Language
- Religion
- Socio-economic status
- Veteran status

Colleges and universities around the country make it a significant part of their mission to promote, support, and celebrate diversity. They have good reason to do so. In order to thrive in the increasingly interconnected 21st century, students need to understand their own background and experience and learn about others. The world is complex and varied; a successful student will learn how to approach complexities with an open mind.

Consider these statistics:

- There are more than 450 languages spoken in the United States (Source: **www.ets.org**)

- About 10% of the U.S. population is foreign-born (Source: U.S. Census **www.census.gov**)

- 40% of American college students are "nontraditional": 25 years old or older. (Source: **studentaid.ed.gov**)

While these statistics give just a glimpse of the diversity in the United States, they provide a starting point for envisioning the college classroom of the 21st century, where students who are foreign-born and those who were born in the United States, 18-year-olds and 36-year-olds, Catholics and Buddhists, students with no financial concerns and students who are struggling to pay for each term learn and work together.

The first step to becoming **culturally competent** (having knowledge of others' cultures, beliefs, perspectives, etc.) is recognizing how one's own culture and background influences one's perspective. Be aware of any stereotypes or prejudices you hold. A **stereotype** is a conventional or oversimplified image or idea. Regional stereotypes in the United States are common: "Midwesterners are ..." and "People from the East Coast are ...". There are positive and negative stereotypes of different groups of people, and these stereotypes accomplish the same thing: They impose a "type" or identity on an individual. **Prejudice** is judging somebody because of a preconceived notion or opinion. ("He is an older student; therefore, he must ...".)

You'll find that if you treat people with respect and as individuals, you'll make meaningful connections and enjoy the similarities as well as differences. College is a gathering of people of different backgrounds, experiences, characteristics, and values. You have an incredible opportunity to connect with and learn from this diverse group of individuals—and to share your own experiences and perspective. **You will probably have opportunities within classes to explore points of view, experiences, and ideas that are unfamiliar to you.** Take advantage of these opportunities as often as possible. Also, **look for ways to get involved and explore diversity on your campus.**

A big part of your education will come from the things you do and learn outside of your academic requirements. You can attend classes, take notes, do the assigned work, and even get high marks, but if you aren't learning from the students and instructors around you, you'll be missing one of the most important aspects of a college education.

It's easy to surround yourself with people who are similar to you, but doing so is limiting. Challenge yourself to recognize and question your assumptions about other people, and you will be amazed at what you find. Students not only learn more about other people when they are in a diverse community; they also learn about themselves.

Keys to Success **Exercises**

1. Describe a time when you demonstrated high self-efficacy: What was the task before you? What conditions do you think led you to feel you were very capable? What was the result?

2. Describe a time when you demonstrated low self-efficacy: What was the task before you? What conditions do you think led you to feel you were incapable? What was the result?

3. In general, do you believe you have a positive perception of self-efficacy? Explain. What steps can you take to maintain or improve your perception of self-efficacy?

4. Follow the tips included in this chapter's goal-setting section to set some personal and academic goals. Explain why each goal is meaningful to you, write out an action plan for each goal, and describe how you plan to stay motivated.

5. Visit your college's multicultural center to learn more about clubs, activities, and resources available on campus and in your community. Choose one event or activity to participate in or learn about that is different and new to you. Either write a two-page reflection on your experience or share your experience with a small group of students in class.

Visit **www.LifeDuringCollege.com**
for more resources and exercises.

Time Management

CHAPTER 14

In the military, you learned to make do with less. Maybe you didn't have all the supplies necessary for a mission or the time allotted for a certain task was simply not enough. Regardless of these constraints, you got creative and found a way to make it work. From getting up early for PT to making it to formation or watch, the military is a structured world where time is a precious resource that must be accounted for.

As a first-year college student you probably have more free time – that is, time you can plan and define for yourself – than ever. On the other hand, with a challenging class load, work demands, and social distractions, it's easy to feel like there aren't enough hours to do what you want to do. Added to this, you also don't have an NCO watching you to ensure that you show up to class or make adequate time in your schedule to complete an assignment. In short, your time is yours and this freedom requires sound responsibility, discipline, and mindfulness.

In the following pages, we'll

- show you how to create a time log
- recommend time management strategies that will help you take control of your time
- reveal common time zappers—and how to avoid them

Your Personal Time Log

In order to manage your time well, you need to know how you currently spend it. Keep track of how you use time for three days—from how long you spend in the shower each day to how many hours you watch television to how many hours you spend sleeping, eating, studying, attending class....you get the picture.

Example of one student's time log:

Time	Activity
8:00 – 8:15 a.m.	Wake up, shower
8:15 – 8:30 a.m.	Get dressed
8:30 – 8:45 a.m.	Check email
8:45 – 9:10 a.m.	Eat breakfast
9:10 – 10:15 a.m.	Study

Keep a small notebook with you so you can write things down

as you do them. Record your activities accurately. (If you're supposed to be studying, but you take a break to check your favorite blog, write it down!) It might seem crazy to take 15 seconds to write down that you just wrote a one-minute email, but those emails and other little tasks add up. All of this data will help you reflect on how you currently spend your time—and, more importantly, help you manage your time realistically and efficiently.

Time Management Strategies

Once you have a sense of how you spend your days, it's time to adjust so that you can get the most out of them.

1. Create a Term Calendar

This calendar serves as a quick reference to all the major events of the term: Exams, assignments, club meetings, family events, appointments, personal projects, visits from friends or family, etc.

Use the right calendar. Your term calendar can be in any form, but it has to be easy to read and use.

Use your syllabi to write in all important due dates, deadlines, and exams.

> **Apps for TimeManagement** **TIP**
> - **Things**
>   (iPhone, iPad, iPod touch)
> - **Checklist Wrangler**
>   (iPhone, iPad, iPod touch)
> - **ToodleDo**
>   (Android, BlackBerry, iPhone, iPad, iPod touch)
> - **Awesome Note**
>   (iPhone, iPad)
> - **A+ TimeTable** (Android)
> - **myHomework** (Kindle Fire, Android, iPhone, iPad)

Review your term calendar regularly—at least once a week.

Resolve conflicts immediately. Even if the conflicts are weeks or months away, it's best to resolve them as soon as you recognize there's a problem.

2. Create a Weekly Schedule

Map out a rough plan for each week on Sunday or Monday. Block out time for all the things you need and want to do. This takes some time but it will save you energy as the week progresses.

Write in all must-dos, such as classes, meetings, and appointments.

Review your term calendar to make sure you don't overlook any deadlines, commitments, or engagements.

Write in some want-to-dos. Schedule time to exercise, meet up with friends, and to do other things that are important to your well-being.

Don't overschedule yourself. Avoid filling up your calendar with every little detail. You want a calendar you can actually live with.

> **Schedules and to-do lists save energy: You won't have to make as many decisions throughout the day if you've got a lot of them mapped out already.**

Sample Weekly Schedule

	Monday	Tuesday	Wednesday	Thursday	Friday
6:30					
7:00					
7:30					
8:00					
8:30					
9:00	Psych 101		Psych 101	Study	Psych 101
9:30					
10:00					
10:30					Study
11:00	Eng Comp	Eng Comp	Eng Comp	Eng Comp	
11:30					
12:00					
12:30			Run w/ Tom		
1:00		Lunch w/Kris			Lunch
1:30					
2:00	Poly Sci	Poly Sci		Poly Sci	Poly Sci
2:30					
3:00			Orientation		
3:30	Workout	Workout			
4:00				Appt. w/ tutor	
4:30				Study	
5:00	Study	Study			
5:30			Span. Club mtg		
6:00					
6:30					
7:00	Dinner	Dinner		Dinner	
7:30					
8:00			Movie @ Kane		
8:30					
9:00		Volleyball		Volleyball	
9:30					
10:00					
10:30					
11:00					
11:30					
12:00					

Visit **www.LifeDuringCollege.com** for more resources and exercises.

3. Create Daily To-Do Lists

The to-do list is not just a goal-setting tool; it can also help you relax. After all, it takes energy to maintain a mental record of what you need and want to do. If everything's in your head, you have to remember things, re-remember them (Now what was I going to do after lunch?), wonder if you've forgotten anything, etc. Write the tasks down and you've conserved some valuable brain real estate. Also, when things are written down you can cross them off, which can be gratifying. Here's how to create a good to-do list:

Refer to your weekly schedule as a starting point. Write down any appointments, tasks, or activities.

Create a realistic list. Recognize your limitations so you don't go to bed each night feeling like you didn't get anything accomplished.

Break larger tasks down into smaller chunks. For example, instead of writing "research paper" or even "begin research paper," write "determine topic for research paper." The University of Minnesota has a cool assignment calculator on its website that can assist this process (**http://www.lib.umn.edu/help/calculator/**).

Time Management Tips

• Set goals and congratulate yourself when you've met them.

• Don't overschedule yourself or over itemize your calendar.

• Break down big tasks into a series of manageable smaller ones.

• Prioritize tasks.

• Do one thing at a time.

• Take action. Get started on major tasks right away.

• Be flexible. Make adjustments as necessary.

Prioritize. An assignment due the following day should get higher priority than something due the next week. An especially challenging task should be allotted more time than those that you can whip through.

Cross off as you go. It's important to see that you've completed what you set out to do. Doing so will keep stress at bay.

Transfer tasks. If you don't get something done, transfer it to the next day's list. If it's truly not a priority it might take a few days to get to it.

Common Time Zappers

The big bad twins of time wasting are procrastination and interruptions.

Procrastination can be a beautiful thing. It has caused late-night junk drawer cleaning and encouraged friends to linger over a dinner conversation long after the food has gone cold. Procrastination can be creative ("I know! I'll take up knitting!") or mundane ("Hmm, now how about this font? Or this one?"). But it can catch up in a bad way. You know it has hit if you're finishing a paper at 7:45 a.m. for an 8:00 a.m. class, or if you're fanning your project to dry the glue on your way to turn it in.

If you tend to put things off, take some time to reflect on *why* you procrastinate. Is it because the assignment seems overwhelming? Is the work difficult to understand? Are there too many distractions? Is procrastination simply a habit? What do you get out of procrastinating? What would be the benefits of not procrastinating? No advice book is effective on its own. However, if you think about your work habits and determine that putting things off increases your stress level, here are some tips to avoid procrastinating:

Create a realistic schedule for completing tasks.

Maintain a positive, motivated attitude towards your work.

Break tasks and projects into manageable blocks, with realistic breaks built in.

Reward yourself for a job well done—and give yourself something to look forward to.

Enlist support. Set goals with a friend so you can help keep each other on track.

Interruptions are the other common time zappers. The world is full of potential interruptions; the trick is to manage them. Here's how:

Just say no. Or at least, just say "later." People will stop by or call and invite you to join them for a meal, a game, a conversation, everything. Get in the habit of letting people know you're busy and telling them when you will be available.

Turn off the phone, TV, computers, etc. If you can't turn the computer off because you need it for schoolwork, make a commitment to ignore the temptations it contains. Every little beep, ping, and ring will distract you from your task and, ultimately, it will take a lot longer to finish the work.

Establish a schedule. Set study hours and let friends, roommates, and family know that those times are off limits.

Get organized. Sometimes it's not others who interrupt us, but our own tendencies toward distraction. Make sure that once you sit down to work you won't be getting up in five minutes to check on something or retrieve something you forgot you need for the assignment.

See Chapter 8 for more information about the effects of interruptions and multitasking, and tips for how to stay focused.

Consider
This ...

The Night Before a Paper is Due Dilemma –
Boots on the Ground Perspective

In the Coast Guard, we spent hours learning how to clear rooms. Rather than conduct an immediate live-fire exercise in the beginning, which would've been dangerous and premature, we walked through a deliberate process that required sound preparation and attention to detail. First, we entered the room as an unarmed team to get an idea of the tactics and footwork that we needed to master. After gaining competence, we progressed to red guns, which allowed us to continue the training safely. Once our team was confident of the process, we finished the exercise with a live-fire that resulted in a safe and smooth evolution. This took place several days after our initial training.

When writing a paper, you need time to develop the fundamentals and structure of what you plan to say. This process may include sifting through your lecture notes and the readings, taking time to think about the material, developing an outline, writing the actual paper, and then revising. If you wait until the final hours before it's due, your best work won't shine through and you'll likely be disappointed with the finished product.

Time Management **Exercises**

1. Keep track of the way you spend your time for three days. Use the sample time log illustrated at the beginning of this chapter, or create one that works well for you. If you really want to see where your time goes, take the data from your three-day log and create a chart.

2. Create a term calendar and a weekly time schedule. Commit to writing daily to-do lists for this week. At the end of the week, review your term calendar and weekly time schedule. What aspects of this exercise were helpful and something you can imagine continuing for the next month? What aspects of this exercise were not helpful?

3. What are **your** most common time zappers? Write down your top five common time zappers and devise a plan to limit the amount of time they take up this week. Make sure you set reasonable expectations for yourself! There's no need to avoid your favorite social media site altogether, for example. Just try spending half the time on it that you usually do. Share your goals with a classmate or friend and report to that same person at the end of the week.

Visit **www.LifeDuringCollege.com**
for more resources and exercises.

Healthy Living

CHAPTER 15

At college, there are a lot of things to distract you from balanced meals and regular sleep habits.

So it might seem comedic for us to include a chapter that advises, among other things, to get a full 7 – 8 hours of sleep a night, to eat healthful foods, to exercise regularly, and to limit stress. Those recommendations seem to apply to another world. College students, after all, regularly get by on only four hours of sleep. Sodium, sugar, and caffeine are considered essential nutrients, and a whole pizza counts as a little late night snack.

Nevertheless, it's worth reviewing the recommendations that mortals live by. (Or should live by, anyway.) The importance of healthy habits cannot be overstated. And, after all, this is a new phase in your life—a perfect time to establish new, healthy habits. When you have a healthy base, it's easy to recover from the occasional very late night or overindulgence.

In this chapter, we'll discuss the importance of

- sleep, including its benefits to mind and body
- healthful eating habits
- exercise, and why you should make it a regular part of your day
- sexual health
- other aspects of physical and mental health

We'll also outline the flip side of health, including

- poor diets and eating disorders
- depression
- disability management and accomodations

Sleep

As a veteran, you've likely functioned on 4 – 5 hours of sleep. You've also heard the recommendations on 7 – 8 hours a night. But why? Why not 7 – 8 hours in little snippets throughout the 24-hour cycle? Or why not 14 hours one night a week and 4 the others?

Consider This ...

Want to avoid the 'Freshman Fifteen'?

Get some sleep! According to the U.S. Department of Health and Human Services, "Studies find that the less people sleep, the more likely they are to be overweight or obese, to develop diabetes, and to prefer eating foods that are high in calories and carbohydrates."

The answer is sleep quality. People need to have consecutive hours of sleep so they can go through the necessary sleep cycles. While you sleep your body and brain are busy releasing hormones, restoring energy, and doing other work that will make you smarter, stronger, and more alert the next day.

Good sleep improves learning, performance, mood, and health. There are countless studies to support the importance of sleep—and that detail the negative effects for those who don't get enough or whose sleep isn't of high quality.

To maintain good sleep habits:

Go to bed and wake up at the same time every day. Erratic sleep patterns can lead to insomnia and other problems.

Nap. Research shows that short naps can actually make you more alert and enhance your performance.

Plan. When you plan well, you can avoid all-nighters. Studying all night won't help you absorb information anyway, so you might as well study efficiently during your alert hours and enjoy your sleep.

Avoid showers, baths, and exercise the hour before bedtime. They are stimulating and make it difficult to get to sleep. Caffeine, alcohol, and some medications also inhibit sleep.

Exercise. Do exercise, but don't do vigorous exercise in the three hours before bedtime as it will keep you awake.

Make your room sleep-friendly. Get the temperature right, minimize light and noise, and make your bed comfortable (and not just an extension of your desk).

Do You Need Less Sleep?

GOOD To KNOW

Many people claim to function just fine on four or five hours of sleep. But they may be fooling themselves. According to a 2009 study published in *Science*, fewer than 5% of us are short sleepers—people who truly need less sleep than the recommended amount.

Eating

You probably have less structure than you're used to these days, which can wreak havoc on your diet. It's no wonder that many first-year college students succumb to the proverbial Freshman Fifteen. The Freshman Fifteen is actually a myth, but most students do gain weight their first year. Men gain an average of 6 pounds and women gain an average of 4 ½ pounds.

The First-Year Student's Sure-Fire Way to Gain Weight

Eat what you want, when you want it

Eat irregularly and erratically

Consume high fat, high calorie, and nutritionally empty foods

Drink beer and other alcoholic beverages

Eat to deal with stress

Don't sleep enough

Skip exercise or get too little exercise

Now, very few people intend to gain weight their first year of college. It just happens, sneaking up ninja-like. The best way to avoid such weight gain is to be aware of your diet and to know the basic facts of good nutrition. You've heard it before, but let's review and make some simple, manageable goals that even the most harried college student can follow reasonably:

Six Easy Nutrition Goals

GOAL #1: Choose a good "default" breakfast. This should be a standard, healthy breakfast that you can eat almost every day. That way you won't have to make decisions about breakfast and you won't end up skipping it—two things that can kill your goal. If you have an early class, breakfast should probably be something simple. Good options: Instant oatmeal, toast with peanut butter, a hearty cereal with milk and a banana, or eggs and fruit.

GOAL #2: Make meals a part of your daily routine so that you don't get ravenously hungry and end up digging into a personal pan pizza.

GOAL #3: Pack healthy snacks (protein bars, almonds, raisins, fruit, etc.) to classes and study sessions.

GOAL #4: Keep a water bottle with you and drink from it regularly. Benefits: You'll stay hydrated; you won't get thirsty and mistake the thirst for hunger; you won't be tempted to drink empty calories; you'll have a place for a cool sticker that the cute student next to you will ask you about and then he or she will ask you what you're doing after class and then….

GOAL #5: Eat 7 or more servings of fresh fruits and vegetables a day. The benefits: You'll get vital nutrients AND you'll be filling up on good things, making the other stuff just a little less tempting.

Goal #6: Read nutrition labels. The cafeteria's chicken pot pie might sound great until you read its stats. Make informed decisions.

There's a lot more to know about nutrition, of course, but these goals can help you start some basic good eating habits. For more information, check into your school's health centers and gyms. You will discover seminars, classes, and support for healthy eating. Also, check out these online resources: **www.mypyramid.gov** and **www.nutrition.gov**.

Eating Disorders

Avoiding the so-called Freshman Fifteen is one issue, but of course it is minor compared to the eating disorders some students develop (or continue) in college. For some students, what begins as a diet and fitness plan turns into anorexia, bulimia, binge eating, or over-exercising. Eating disorders are serious and, unfortunately, common at college, where triggers like pressure, stress, and anxiety are part of daily life.

According to the U.S. Department of Health and Human Services:

> **Eating disorders are more than just a problem with food. Food is used to feel in control of other feelings that may seem overwhelming. For example, starving is a way for people with anorexia to feel more in control of their lives and to ease tension, anger, and anxiety. Purging and other behaviors to prevent weight gain are ways for people with bulimia to feel more in control of their lives and to ease stress and anxiety.**

Every college has resources to help students who develop an eating disorder or who want to help a friend whom they think might have an eating disorder. Hotlines, support groups, seminars, counseling, and medical intervention are available at many colleges. If you suspect you have an eating disorder or are prone to developing one, it is important that you seek professional help immediately. Also, be a good friend: If someone you know seems to be struggling with an eating disorder, discuss your concerns with a counselor at your college. He or she will have resources and advice that can help you get your friend help.

Eating Disorders Affect Men, Too

40% of people with binge eating disorder are men
10 – 15% of people with anorexia or bulimia are male

Source: **www.eatingdisorderinfo.org**

Exercise – Don't Throw Out the PT Gear!

While in the military, physical training was a regular part of the daily routine for health, morale, and mission readiness. Although you may no longer get up at zero dark thirty to run 5 miles while calling cadence, maintaining a regular PT schedule will work wonders for your life during college.

The American College of Sports Medicine and the American Heart Association's minimum recommendation for healthy adults who wish to maintain their health and weight is simple: Get at least 3 – 5 cardio workouts each week and at least two strength training workouts.

Still need more convincing on why you should pull out the PT gear?

Exercise:

- increases energy
- helps you get a better night's sleep
- reduces stress
- increases self-confidence
- reduces your risk of heart disease, high blood pressure, and diabetes
- makes you look and feel great
- is fun!

Here are some ways to make exercise a regular part of your life in college:

Schedule time to exercise. If it's a priority—and it should be—it needs to be on your calendar and as fixed as an appointment you would make with another person.

Develop a realistic exercise plan that you can follow. It's better to work out half an hour a day six days a week for a semester than to work out three hours each day for a week, then give it up.

Join an intramural sports team. Have fun, meet people, and stay in shape.

Find an exercise partner. Having a friend who commits to exercise with you is a great way to stay motivated and on track. (Sometimes, literally on the track!)

Choose to move. Walk or bike to class instead of taking the bus or driving. Walk up stairs instead of taking the elevator. Choose dancing or bowling rather than watching a movie. Play football instead of watching football on TV.

> **99 bottles of beer on the waistline...** *Good To Know*
>
> To work off the number of calories (153) in a typical bottle of beer, you would need to:
>
> Jog for 18 minutes
> OR
> Bike for 23 minutes
> OR
> Swim for 13 minutes!
>
> For more calorie/exercise calculations, check out www.calorieking.com

Enroll in a PE class. This option is extra-motivating (you can't not show up to a class, right?) and will give you a chance to try new activities.

Take advantage of your college's resources. You have access to more activities, trips, gyms, trainers, and organized sports than you'll ever have in your life.

Check with the community. Many communities host 5K, 10K, half and full marathons along with mud runs and other obstacle based fitness activities. Want to share the love? Grab a few friends from class or the veterans club and form a team.

Sexual Health

Of course, one aspect of your personal health is your relationships with others. If you are sexually active, you need to take extra precautions to keep yourself healthy and to prevent an unplanned pregnancy. According to The National Campaign to Prevent Teen and Unplanned Pregnancy, 3 in 10 females in the U.S. get pregnant at least once by age 20, and an unplanned pregnancy increases the risk of a student dropping out of college. Yet, many college students report that they do not use birth control on a regular basis. Some even persist in

> Here are some online resources and quizzes that can help you increase your sexual IQ:
>
> **www.studentsexlife.org**
> **www.smartersex.org**
> **www.thenationalcampaign.org**

believing myths (for example, twenty percent of guys believe that having sex standing up prevents pregnancy). To find out more about contraception effectiveness and options, including facts, statistics, and resources, head to **www.smartersex.org**.

Sexually transmitted infections (STIs) is another topic college students need to know about. After all, according to the American Social Health Association, 1 in 5 people in the United States has an STI and two-thirds of STIs occur in people under 25. What's more, many people who have an STI do not know they have it, so they unknowingly pass it on to others. For example, according to www.smartersex.org, 80% of the people who have herpes do not know they have it. If you are sexually active, you owe it to yourself and your partner to be well-informed.

Stress

Stress can be a positive. It can motivate and encourage creativity, for instance. On the other hand, if not managed well, stress can cause mental, physical, and emotional strain. Left unchecked, high stress can lead to health problems such as anxiety, depression, weight gain, headaches, and high blood pressure. Stress is inevitable, but there are strategies you can adopt to minimize its impact. Here are some:

1) Recognize the signs of stress, which may include

- Dramatic weight loss or gain
- Headaches
- Fatigue
- Diarrhea
- Problems sleeping
- Muscle tightness or spasms
- Frustration, nervousness, irritability, and mood swings
- Lack of interest in things you used to enjoy
- Loss of concentration
- Forgetfulness
- A feeling of being overwhelmed

2) Know the common stressors of college life:

- Exams and assignments
- Grades
- Studying
- Relationships
- Time demands and scheduling conflicts
- Uncertainty about the future
- Finances

3) Get a handle on stress:

Practice good organization and time management. Planning well will help you avoid situations that lead to stress, such as forgotten appointments, overdue assignments, and lost items.

GOOD TO KNOW

Negative Impacts on Academic Success

Students reported the following factors as negatively impacting their academic performance:

Stress:	30.7%
Sleep Difficulties:	21.4%
Anxiety:	20.8%
Cold/Flu/Sore Throat:	16.7%
Work:	15.5%
Depression:	13.2%
Internet Use/Computer Games:	13%

Source: ACHA-NCHAII Survey, Spring 2013

Shift your perspective. What will this stressful event feel like a week from now? Next year? In 5 years?

Break overwhelming projects into smaller, more manageable tasks. Instead of cleaning your entire room in one day, for example, set the goal to clean out the closet one day, and the rest of the living space the following day.

Stay healthy. (See the sections on diet and exercise earlier in this chapter.)

Take a break. When you're feeling overwhelmed, take time to think about it and do other things.

Be good to yourself. Don't beat yourself up over things. Make sure you reflect on the things you do right and focus on how you can use that self-knowledge in the future.

Play. Take time to have fun. It will release stress and give you perspective on the things that are causing your anxiety.

Get help if you need it. Just because stress is common doesn't mean it's too trivial to discuss with a counselor. If it's negatively affecting you, seek professional advice.

Illness

The stressful, often erratic college lifestyle, combined with close contact with many other people, can make college students especially prone to illness. Some, like colds, are a mere inconvenience. Others, such as hepatitis and meningitis, can be life threatening.

Reduce your risk of illness by taking the following measures:

Make sure your immunizations are up to date.

Cover your coughs and sneezes, and wash your hands often.

Don't share eating and drinking utensils or toothbrushes and hairbrushes.

Handle food with care. If you're not sure how long that yogurt's been sitting out, err on the safe side and toss it. For food safety guidelines, including storage times for refrigerated food, go to **www.foodsafety.gov.**

Don't overuse antibiotics. Use antibiotics only when necessary and only when prescribed to you. If you are prescribed antibiotics, finish the entire course of the drug to ensure that the illness has been truly cured.

See a doctor or physician's assistant when necessary. Ignoring symptoms won't make them go away and it won't make the underlying condition any easier or cheaper to treat.

Practice safe sex. Sexually transmitted diseases (STDs) are very common among college populations. Abstinence is the only foolproof way to avoid an STD, but if you decide to engage in sexual activity, protect yourself from unnecessary risk.

Depression

Over 30% of college students report they have felt "so depressed it was difficult to function" at some point in the school year (Source: The ACHA-NCHAII, Spring 2013). College students are particularly vulnerable to depression because of all the life-altering changes and transitions they are going through. For a first-year student veteran, dealing with the stress of an intensive academic schedule, or juggling other important responsibilities such as work and family commitments, can quickly accelerate the stress factor.

Depression can be trigged by an event like the loss of a loved one, serious physical illness or injury, a failed relationship, or a series of bad grades. Often, depression is inherited and individuals with a family history of depression may be more likely to suffer from depression themselves. Sometimes depression isn't attributable to any particular cause, but is brought on by a combination of circumstances.

Need to Talk?
Need Help?

Veteran's Crisis Line
1-800-273-TALK
(800-273-8255)

The good news is that depression is a treatable illness. If you are experiencing any of the following symptoms, you should seek help from your college physician, counselor, or from the Department of Veterans Affairs:

- Persistent sad, anxious, or "empty" mood
- Feelings of hopelessness or pessimism
- Feelings of guilt, worthlessness, helplessness
- Loss of interest or pleasure in activities you once enjoyed
- Decreased energy, fatigue, feeling slowed down
- Difficulty concentrating, remembering, or making decisions
- Insomnia, early-morning awakening, or oversleeping
- Appetite changes and/or weight loss or weight gain
- Thoughts of death or suicide
- Restlessness, irritability
- Persistent physical symptoms that do not respond to treatment, such as headaches, digestive disorders, and chronic pain

Disability Management

In the military a disabling condition can mean the difference between doing your job and sitting on the sidelines. Although it's not uncommon for service members to have a range of invisible and visible wounds and injuries, as a group, veterans rarely identify as disabled. Added to this, military culture often encourages one to confront a disability with a "suck it up and drive on" attitude. In other words, to just deal with it and push forward.

In the current conflicts in the Middle East, Traumatic Brain Injury, or TBI, is considered the signature wound of battle. Even a minor head injury can create all sorts of havoc for a student veteran. For example, the rigors of studying and preparing for an exam are stressful enough. Now add memory issues, migraines, and sleep disturbances on top of this. Multiply these barriers by four or five classes and you've got a real problem on your hands. The good news is that most colleges have been assisting students with disabilities for decades and are well positioned to provide individualized services and accommodations.

Accommodations

An accommodation is a modification or adjustment to instructional methods in a course, program, service, activity or facility that enables students with a documented disability to have an equal opportunity. An equal opportunity means an opportunity to attain the same level of performance or to enjoy equal benefits and privileges as are available to students without a disability. Although each college varies, common accommodations provided through a Disability Office include

- Priority registration
- Note-taking services
- Text conversion

- Testing accommodations, such as extended time on exams and distraction-free testing environments
- Educating students of their rights and responsibilities as a person with a disability
- Low-cost or free neuro-psychological screenings

Good To Know

National Crisis Hotlines

Important numbers to know if you or a friend needs information or help:

Cutting and Self-Abuse
1-800-DONT-CUT (1-800-366-8288) (Self Abuse Finally Ends organization)

Eating Disorders
1-800-931-2237 (National Eating Disorder Organization)

Pregnancy
1-800-230-PLAN (1-800-230-7526) (Planned Parenthood Hotline)

Rape, Sexual Abuse, and Incest
1-800-656-HOPE (1-800-656-4673) (RAINN Rape Crisis Hotline)

Suicide Hotline
1-800-273-TALK (1-800-273-8255)

Healthy Living **Exercises**

1. Keep track of your sleep for a week. How much sleep do you average per night? Is it high quality sleep? Do you feel well rested after a night's sleep?

2. Tour your campus's athletic and exercise facilities. What are their hours of operation? What kinds of classes are available?

3. Visit your college's counseling center and health center. What kinds of resources are available in each center? What are their hours? How does one go about making an appointment?

4. If a friend exhibited signs of a possible eating disorder, what steps would you take to get him or her help? Discuss with a group.

5. If a friend exhibited signs of depression, what steps would you take to get him or her help? Discuss with a group.

Visit **www.LifeDuringCollege.com**
for more resources and exercises.

Social Media and You

CHAPTER 16

What is power? Consider the whistleblowers who can, with a few anonymous posts, leak information that shakes up a huge corporation or a government. Or the community that, after being devastated by a natural disaster, rallies and organizes assistance through tweets and Facebook posts. Or the college student who can, with a green screen and a cheap camera, transform himself into a popular YouTube movie critic. Thank social media for all of that.

As with all forms of great power, there's a flip side. Social media makes it possible to connect with loved ones, acquaintances, and strangers who share your interests; it also makes it possible for other people to paint a one-sided picture of you that's hard to control. It allows information to spread quickly, but that information might be incorrect or damaging. Social media is also quite deceptive: the "little guy" can turn him or herself into a powerful voice for his or her cause; the bully can be a jerk 24/7 to a huge audience. And, of course, social media can be addictive and a waste of time.

In this chapter, we'll discuss

- connecting with friends and family via social media
- building a good online presence—now and into your future
- risks of social media
- ways to improve privacy and security online

Connecting via Social Media

As a 21st century college student, you have broad reach. You can connect easily with all sorts of people and groups and maintain those connections. It can also give you a platform for building relationships with other students, instructors, and even alumni.

Incidentally, one challenge you'll have as a first-year student might be connecting to your new environment with the people right next to you. You know, the *physical* ones.

Social media also makes it simple to stay in touch with everyone at home along with friends and battle buddies who are deployed or underway.

Your (Online) Identity

If you are like 94% of your peers, you already have an online identity. You've probably been using Instagram and Twitter for years and have already built an online presence. But here's a concept many people who use social media are just beginning to grasp: FOREVER. Your online presence will stick around for a lot longer than the technology you're using to drive it. There's no shame in acting childish or saying things we wish we hadn't, but the Internet isn't a forgiving place. Things stick around. No need to panic, but there are some things you need to know to keep your personal identity and your online identity under control.

In this section we'll discuss how to manage your online presence so that it helps you in the future rather than holds you back.

First, take stock of your current online profile. Google yourself to see what others can easily find out about you. See anything interesting? If you end up with a few innocuous results (your little league batting average or a graduation picture, for instance), you are in a great position, as you can simply monitor your online presence and make sure nothing gets linked to your name that you don't want. You'll also want to build on that presence, which we'll get to in a moment.

Second, delete or bury content, if necessary. If you do have blog posts, pictures, or other items online that could potentially embarrass you or limit your chances of finding and keeping a job in the future, simply delete them, if possible. It's not likely that you can remove the images or content from every source, but you can try to bury it by increasing favorable content. For instance, some people use LinkedIn, Twitter, or Pinterest, because activity on those websites makes their most relevant and recent content most visible. It's no different than what many companies do to help their brand. You can do the same thing.

Another way to bury negative items is to create a new website or blog and add to it regularly.

Finally, think about your future online identity. What do you want future connections, colleagues, employers and potential employers to learn about you when they search for you online? They do check. You can build up a professional presence with LinkedIn and Twitter and following those organizations that relate to your academic interests. For example, a student passionate about marine biology might become a digital advocate for the group Ocean Conservancy. Connecting with organizations you're genuinely interested in will keep you up to date on the latest news in your field and might also lead you to internship opportunities. Who knows? Your social media savvy might compel the organizations you're interested in to hire you to manage their own social media presence.

Don't worry if you don't have your professional goals all figured out at this stage. If you do know what you want to do when you graduate from college, you can start building a more specific professional presence online now. If you aren't sure what you want to do next semester much less in four years, you can still establish a foundational professional presence online now.

Privacy and Security

What are the risks of social media? Our engagement on social media starts with taking a risk: we give up certain privacy in order to connect with others or have access to something we want. Once you're in, it's simply a matter of limiting or increasing your risk.

Behaviors that increase your risk:

- Posting personal information, including phone number, address, and date of birth

- Posting personal plans (for example, when you're leaving town, which route you're traveling)

- Sharing images and text that you'd be embarrassed about if they got out or existed forever (assume both will happen)

- Password and PIN laziness: As we discuss in Chapter 4, you want strong passwords even if they're hard to remember

- Not using privacy settings and not paying attention when privacy settings change

- Clicking before thinking. If people paused before clicking, there would be fewer victims of scams (Best Buy is giving away free televisions!!! Click "like" and submit your name and email address to claim yours!!) and fewer apologies necessary (Sorry about previous tweet. My info was wrong.)

Unfortunately, there are some things out of our control entirely. People have had their lives turned upside down by all sorts of jerks, some of them criminal and some not. For example, in addition to the scammers, phishers, and catfishers, there are people who create social media accounts in others' names and use the platform to bully. There are others who repost sexy or obscene pictures (real or edited) and try to charge the victim money to remove them.

It's revolutionary, evolving, pervasive, and powerful. While social media modes change quickly, they all satisfy a basic human need: to communicate. Unlike the days when humans gathered around the fire pit, however, the communication

Make an Impression with Online Posts or Tweets

Consider This ...

Job recruiters are impressed by:

- Affiliations with professional organizations
- Volunteerism

Job recruiters are turned off by:

- References to drugs, alcohol, and sex
- Rude or disparaging remarks about others
- Poor grammar and spelling mistakes
- Self-centered posts

Source: Jobvite, 2012

now is easily replicated and archived forever. We have just hundreds of cave paintings from early humans, and millions of silly pet videos from modern humans. Whether you use social media to entertain or to inform, whether you use it to create or curate, use it wisely.

Carnegie Mellon researchers found that public information easily found online can be used to predict an individual's social security number.

Source: Carnegie Mellon, 2009

GOOD TO KNOW

Social Media **Exercises**

1. Google yourself and note the top twenty hits your search yields. What would someone else learn about you if they were to Google your name?

2. Consider your social media use. How much of it is dedicated to consuming content? To creating content? To curating content?

3. Working with a small group of classmates, discuss the use of social media in your classes: How are professors integrating social media tools? How are students using it to work together? How are students using it to learn or conduct research?

4. Working with a small group of classmates, discuss what you see as an up-and-coming social media site or platform. What makes it appealing? What are its potential uses?

Visit **www.LifeDuringCollege.com** for more resources and exercises.

Housing Options

CHAPTER 17

Most first-year college students live on campus. In fact, some colleges insist on it, because it provides a support system and safeguards as students become accustomed to living on their own away from home. However, unless they really loved living in the barracks and sharing a bathroom, most veterans choose to live off campus. This chapter will walk you through housing options and related issues, including:

- choosing housing: on- vs. off-campus housing
- finding the right apartment
- understanding your lease
- tips for moving in and out
- Service members Civil Relief Act

Pros and Cons of On-Campus Living

On-campus housing is maintained, operated, and subsidized by your college. While most on-campus housing is located on the campus, some colleges—especially those in urban areas—maintain housing facilities on properties that are not actually part of the campus. Common types of on-campus housing include:

Residence Halls
Residence halls are usually multi-story buildings featuring rooms that are shared by two, possibly three, roommates. Each residence hall floor usually has a kitchen and living area as well as a suite of bathrooms that is shared by all the residents of a floor.

Suites
Some dorms are divided into suites—apartment-like sections of a building. A suite may consist of two to four bedrooms connected by a common living area with a kitchen and shared bathroom.

Student Apartments or Townhouses
These are living situations modeled after off-campus housing. They are just like an apartment or townhouse and are usually very popular. (Hmm, perhaps because you don't have to share a bathroom with forty other people?)

Greek Living

If you choose to join a sorority or fraternity, you may have additional options, as many of these organizations maintain houses or residence hall floors on campus. Students who choose Greek living live alongside their "brothers" or "sisters" in settings that can range from mansion-like homes with a full staff to run-down, overcrowded houses.

Family Housing

Most colleges offer housing specifically designed for students who are married and/or who have children. Family housing is often similar to student apartments or townhouses, and may include amenities like a day care center and playground.

When you do have a choice of whether or not to live on campus, consider these pros and cons:

Pros	Cons
CENTRAL LOCATION: On-campus housing is close to everything you need—your classes, the dining hall, campus recreation, etc.	**NO CHOICE OF ROOMMATES:** Many colleges assign roommates, though some will allow student input in the process.
NO COMMUTE: You can walk, bike, or take a campus shuttle to get around easily.	**FEWER OPTIONS:** Depending on your college, you may have a limited list of living arrangements in comparison to off-campus options.
SERVICES: On-campus living usually includes conveniences such as custodial services, trash pick-up, pest extermination, and repairs.	
SUPPORT: You will have a handy support network of resident assistants and advisors, the campus housing office, and other resources.	**LIMITED PRIVACY:** Shared facilities and group living is part of the on-campus living experience—and one you may not love.
COST-EFFECTIVE: Once you add up all the services included in your housing fees and subtract the hidden costs of living off campus (for example, commuting costs, grocery bills, cleaning supplies, etc.), living on campus can be more cost-effective, especially if your college is in an up-scale or urban area.	**MEAL LIMITATIONS:** If your housing includes a meal plan, you might tire of the restrictions of on-campus eating—hours of operation and choices of food.
	RULES AND REGULATIONS: To maintain order, protect property, and ensure students' safety, colleges set and enforce all kinds of rules and regulations.
ALL-INCLUSIVE: You will not have to worry about bills for heating, air-conditioning, electricity, water, gas, or sewer. Many colleges also offer free Internet and cable.	**LIMITATIONS ON GUESTS AND PETS:** Most campus housing bans pets, and many have rules about how many visitors are permitted.
SAFETY: Crime occurs everywhere, but on-campus housing generally has more security resources available.	**PARKING RESTRICTIONS:** Parking on campus near your residence hall may be restricted and/or inconvenient.
RESERVES & NATIONAL GUARD: For students affiliated with the Reserves or National Guard, on-campus housing contracts are easy to break should you be called up to active duty and forced to withdraw from school. Many colleges have a formal policy to handle activations, so be sure to check with your Veterans Office for more information.	

GOOD TO KNOW

Theme Houses and Other On-Campus Anomalies

Here are some of the options for students wanting a particular on-campus living situation:

Designated residence halls, such as Substance Free residence halls or Quiet residence halls

Designated floors, such as The Scholars' Floor or The French Floor

Theme Houses, such as

- Global Environment Theme House (UC Berkeley)
- Women in Science and Engineering Theme House (UC Berkeley)
- House of the Living Arts (Wheaton)
- International House (many colleges)

Pros and Cons of Off-Campus Housing

Your options for off-campus housing are varied and range from leasing an apartment with a roommate in an apartment complex, to renting a home with a group of friends, to renting a room in a family's home. Off-campus living may seem like a dream after a year of having three meals a day at the college cafeteria and enduring the noise of dozens of other students at all hours of the night. However, off-campus living has both an up and a down side:

Pros	Cons
MAY BE LESS EXPENSIVE: On-campus housing includes a lot of services, which may make it more expensive than your off-campus options.	**MAY BE INCONVENIENTLY LOCATED:** You'll be—by definition—off campus, and may have to trek quite a way to get to your classes.
CHOICE: You get to choose where to live, your roommate(s), and what kind of living situation fits you best.	**MORE MAINTENANCE:** Some landlords require that their tenants mow the lawn. Others will expect you to deal with some problems—such as cockroaches—that arise. The expectations will depend on the situation, but you'll certainly have more maintenance with an off-campus situation.
SPACE AND AMENITIES: You might get a more spacious apartment, and one with more bells and whistles.	
PRIVACY: Because you can choose your living situation, you can elect to have a private bedroom and even a private bathroom. Also, it may be easier to find quiet time to study, sleep, and relax.	**MORE RESPONSIBILITY:** No custodians. No oversight. You will need to remember to take out the trash, clean the fridge, and pay the electric bill.
INDEPENDENCE: Fewer rules = more freedom.	**HIDDEN EXPENSES:** Toilet paper, cleaning supplies, groceries, commuting costs, your own furniture—the costs add up fast.
PETS AND VISITORS ARE WELCOME (possibly): Many landlords maintain restrictions on pets, but some will allow your furry or feathered friends. And speaking of friends...in off-campus housing you won't have someone standing over your shoulder counting how many visitors come by.	**COMMUTING:** If your off-campus home is not close to campus, you will have the added hassle of commuting.
	LESS SUPPORT: Off-campus housing does not come with a resident advisor or campus housing office. Some landlords may be difficult to work with, and you'll be on your own for any negotiations or issues.

Finding the Right Apartment

If you do decide to move off campus, you'll need to figure out exactly what kind of apartment you want. Sit down with your roommate(s) and make a list of the features and services that are essential to all of you, as well as a list of those things you'd like but don't really need, and the things you'd like to avoid. Then set a price range you can afford. Here are some things to think about:

Location: How close do you want to be to campus? To grocery stores? To the bus or subway line?

Safety: What areas of town are considered safe? Are the units of the apartment well maintained and up to code?

Size: How many bedrooms and bathrooms do you need? How big of a kitchen will suit your lifestyle?

Features: Do you want a place with a yard? A balcony? Air conditioning? Charm?

Amenities: What kinds of things can you not live without? A laundry room? Cable television? A security system? A pool or workout facility?

Rules: Every landlord and apartment complex has its own rules. Do the rules of the apartment you're considering match your lifestyle?

Furnished or unfurnished: You may have the option of renting a furnished apartment, which can offset the cost of living off campus. Do you need furniture? Are you happy with the furniture that's provided?

What do others have to say? Get good intel by checking with other veterans about recommended places to live. Also, do research online. Many websites, such as Yelp and Google Reviews, provide thorough information about apartments and leasing companies, along with tenants' reviews.

After you and your roommates agree on the kind of apartment you want, it's time to start looking. Check out the classified section of the newspaper, Craigslist and other Internet sites, local apartment search services or property management companies, and bulletin boards on campus and around town. Also, drive or bike around town to get a feel for the different neighborhoods and to find potential rentals that haven't been listed yet.

Negotiating with a Landlord and Signing a Lease

Remember the law of supply and demand? It is about to have a direct effect on your life. If there are lots of apartments available in your college community, you will be able to leverage a better deal. If not, you will have to compete with other renters and will need to compromise. One thing you can do to give yourself more leverage is to maintain an excellent credit score, as your credit rating affects your ability to lease as well as the amount of deposit required and the rent price.

GOOD TO KNOW

Check with Your College's Housing Office

Many colleges have a liaison or formal office that works with nontraditional students on housing matters. These offices are helpful for identifying places to live based on budget and individual needs. Some even maintain lists of landlords and leasing companies in addition to reading over and providing guidance on your lease.

Here are a few things you can do to negotiate a better rental deal, even in a scarce market:

Sign an extended lease. If you know you love the property and can commit to staying in it for longer than the minimum lease, let the landlord or property management company know. Landlords love the stability of having good tenants stay for over a year and yours may give you a reduction in rent or security deposit in exchange for signing an extended lease.

Know the rental market. Research the going rental rate for apartments in your area and what kinds of amenities and features you can get for what kinds of prices. Don't be afraid to talk with a landlord about what other complexes or buildings are charging or offering, and to negotiate a better rental rate.

Haggle the deposit. The deposit is one area where landlords may be willing to make allowances because it will, most likely, be returned to you at the end of your rental agreement. Ask if your deposit can be reduced or paid in increments over several months.

Don't just think money. Reducing your rent is ideal, but you may also consider asking the landlord for other allowances, like replacing the fridge or repainting.

Consider asking for a month-to-month lease. Ask the landlord if you can extend your lease on a month-to-month basis once the terms of the original lease are up. This can give you flexibility in the future and help you save on the costs of putting a security deposit down on a new apartment and moving again.

After you have come to an agreement with the landlord on the terms of your rental, go over the written lease very carefully to make sure it reflects your agreement. Before you sign your lease:

Read it carefully. You should ask if you can take the lease home to review it in private. This will give you time to read it word for word—and to enlist the help of a more experienced friend or family member if you need it.

Highlight any concerns and ask for clarification. If there is anything in the lease you do not understand, that concerns you, or that you feel contradicts your oral agreement, highlight that section and insist that your landlord clarify it. In some cases, he or she will have to revise the document before you sign.

Make sure your written lease is identical to your oral agreement. If your landlord promised you new carpet, make sure it's written down. If she said she would waive the pet fee, make sure it's written down.

Moving In and Moving Out

Some college students end up in legal wrangles with landlords or former landlords, which is inconvenient and expensive. Protect yourself by taking the following precautions:

Have a question about your rights as a tenant? *TIP*

Go to your state's attorney general's website to search for tenant rights.

When Moving In:
Conduct a thorough walk-through before moving in. Inspect every aspect and feature in the apartment and make a detailed list of its imperfections: stains, holes, outlets that don't function, broken windows or mirrors, crooked cabinets, nonworking appliances, etc. Ask your landlord to sign your completed list, and then make a copy for each of you.

Make sure it meets your standards. If the apartment has not been cleaned, repaired, or doesn't meet the specifications outlined in your lease, inform the landlord and request that the necessary adjustments be made immediately.

When Moving Out:
Conduct a thorough walk-through with your landlord or the property manager before you move out so he/she can indicate any potential problems, such as damage or alterations.

Have your landlord sign off on a statement outlining what you will be charged for, if anything, and stating when and how your deposit will be returned to you. This is a critical step—students have been surprised by bills for damage many months after they vacated an apartment.

Leave it like you found it. It's good manners and it makes sense to leave the property in as good of shape as you received it. First, you want to establish a good list of references for future rentals. Second, you want to recoup all the money you put down as a deposit.

Special Circumstances

The possibilities are endless, so we'll cover a few of the most common special circumstances you might encounter:

Free-rent promotions. In a saturated market, apartment complexes and landlords will compete for your money. You will see all sorts of promotional programs, including free rent for a certain number of months. Read the fine print and ask the important questions. If you're satisfied that it's a genuine deal, go for it!

Special discounts. Some landlords and property managers offer special discounts to veterans and their family members, employees of specific companies, or members of particular groups. Check to see if that's the case in your new apartment, and ask if the special discount applies to you.

Bartering. If a landlord just has a few properties, he or she might be willing to exchange services for reductions in rent. You might landscape, paint, or do other work and save some much-needed cash.

Subleasing. Because college students are not always able to fulfill the full term of their rental agreements, there may be a variety of subleasing opportunities available to you. Subleasing can sometimes be a good deal because the original renter may be in a tight spot and willing to rent the property for less than he or she is paying. Also, you might not have to pay a deposit in a subleasing situation.

Servicemembers Civil Relief Act (SCRA). For members of the National Guard and Reserves, the Servicemembers Civil Relief Act provides a wide range of protections, including a provision to terminate your lease, when called to active duty. If you find yourself needing to break your lease due to activation, check with Legal Services and the Veterans Office at your college for assistance.

Where to Live **Exercises**

1. With a partner or in a small group, review the two pros and cons lists at the beginning of this chapter. What pros and cons would you add to the on-campus list? What pros and cons would you add to the off-campus list?

2. Create a list of the things you would need, want, and not want in a rental property.

Must have	Want to have	Must Not have

3. Do a little field work to figure out: 1) Where you can find out about housing availabilities in your community, 2) Areas of the community where you would like to live, 3) The price range of off-campus living options, and 4) Where you can find information about the landlord/tenant laws in your state or city.

Visit **www.LifeDuringCollege.com** for more resources and exercises.

Health Insurance

CHAPTER 18

We know this chapter would be voted "Most Likely to be Skipped Over" if a contest were held. We considered titling it Human Sexuality or How to Guarantee a 4.0 just to get your attention, but ultimately decided to go for a more subtle (and honest) approach: HEALTH INSURANCE IS REALLY IMPORTANT.

Leaving the military also meant leaving behind many benefits that you likely took for granted, such as full health coverage. For an active and fit veteran, injury and illness is something for another generation, like dentures and early dinners. You're not alone if you feel that way. In fact, your age group is least likely to hold health insurance, which is partly due to a belief that health insurance is an optional expense. As of 2014, health insurance is a requirement for most Americans. But even when it's not required, it should be a priority. After all, a catastrophic illness or injury could sideline you physically and financially for years.

This chapter will cover

- the importance of health insurance
- health insurance options
- the Department of Veterans Affairs
  Health Care System

The Importance of Health Insurance

Health insurance is a must. Even if you are young and healthy, it is an enormous risk to go without health coverage. Taking such a risk—even for a few months—could have devastating consequences. The out-of-pocket cost of a broken ankle is over $1,500. Going to the ER for a sore throat, getting tested, and being told to go home and get some rest will run you about $500. (Of course, avoiding the ER when you do have a serious illness can cost even more.) And these examples are small potatoes next to catastrophic illnesses, which can easily rack up tens and even hundreds of thousands of dollars.

> **Yes, You Need Health Insurance** *Consider This ...*
>
> 1 in 6 young adults has a chronic illness, such as diabetes or asthma.
>
> Over 23% of young adults had at least one emergency room visit in 2011.
>
> Source: US Dept. of Health and Human Services; Centers for Disease Control and Prevention

Note: *Under the Affordable Care Act, often called Obamacare, health insurance is mandatory for the vast majority of the population. Individuals who don't carry coverage will be fined. Exemptions to the mandate include members of some Indian tribes and individuals making less than $10,000 per year.*

There are several options for health insurance coverage for a first-year college student. One possibility is that you're still covered by your parents' health insurance. If this is the case, you are probably insured by either a Health Maintenance Organization (HMO) or a Preferred Provider Organization (PPO).

HMOs provide health care through a network of doctors, hospitals, and medical professionals. Participants pay a monthly premium in exchange for the HMO's comprehensive care. In order to access full benefits, participants must seek care from in-network primary care physicians and must have a referral in order to see a specialist. HMO members can usually go to out-of-network providers, but they have to pay more out of pocket to do so.

PPOs have a network of preferred healthcare providers, but participants may elect to seek care from a physician outside the network if they are willing to pay more. Unlike HMOs, PPOs generally allow participants to access specialists without a referral.

> **The Affordable Care Act of 2010 requires insurance companies to cover their subscribers' children through the age of 26.**

If your parents have health insurance, it is probably an HMO, PPO, or some variation on the two. More importantly, you can be covered on their policy up to age 26. In Illinois, as a veteran, you can be covered under your parents up to age 30. However, if you live some distance away from home you might be out of network, which means you might not have the same coverage. This means that, while you may have relatively small co-payment requirements at your regular doctor's office back at home, any doctor in your new town will not be a preferred provider. Therefore, your share of the cost of the visit might be quite higher than back at home. To complicate matters, coverage varies from plan to plan and state to state. The best course of action is to call your health insurance company before you move to find out exactly how much coverage you'll have at college, and what you'll need to do to access that coverage. Keep a file of important customer service numbers and preferred providers in your new location.

If you have insurance through your parents' plan, do the following BEFORE the term gets rolling: *TIP*

- Make sure you have a copy of the insurance card
- Find out which providers in the area your insurance will cover
- Know how to access coverage, what kinds of preventive care are available, how to obtain required approvals, and how to file a claim
- Know what to do in case of an emergency

DON'T WAIT! If you get sick or hurt, the last thing you want to do is try to figure out how to navigate your insurance plan.

GOOD TO KNOW If you are covered by your parents' plan, they will know any time a visit is billed to their insurance.

It's much more fun to decorate your apartment and explore the campus, but take care of health insurance business right away so you don't have to deal with it when you're sick or injured.

If your parents do not have health insurance, or if the insurance they have doesn't cover you adequately in your new town, you have other options to explore:

University health insurance plans: Colleges usually contract with insurance companies to offer basic student health insurance plans. These plans have limited coverage. For instance, they often exclude routine care and they might limit catastrophic coverage to $50,000. On the other hand, student health insurance is usually quite inexpensive and can come in more than handy when you have an illness or sustain an injury. You might want to enroll in the student health insurance even if you are already covered on your parents' plan, especially if your parents' plan does not offer extensive coverage.

> **The American Academy of Pediatrics suggests you pack the following:**
>
> *TIP*
>
> - A complete health record
> - A list of medicines you take
> - A list of your allergies, if any
> - A list of any past medical problems
> - A list of any special needs you may have
> - Your immunization record
> - Proof of health insurance
>
> Source: The American Academy of Pediatrics (www.aap.org)

Federal or state insurance exchange: As of 2013, individuals may purchase affordable health care through state or federal health care exchanges. These online marketplaces offer side-by-side comparisons of various plans for comprehensive health insurance. People who make under a certain amount qualify for tax credit subsidies. Go to www.healthcare.gov to find out what's available to you.

Catastrophic coverage: The insurance exchanges offer catastrophic coverage for people who want to pay a very low premium and a high deductible. If you sign up for catastrophic coverage you'll be eligible for just a few preventative visits a year. Catastrophic coverage is better than not having health insurance, but it just protects you from, well, catastrophes.

Medicaid: If your family is low-income and you are still a dependent, you might be eligible for insurance coverage through Medicaid, which is a federal assistance program.

Veterans Affairs Health Care

As a veteran, you are fortunate to have access to VA Health Care. If you have other forms of health care coverage, such as a private insurance plan, Medicare, Medicaid or TRICARE, you can continue to use VA services along with these plans.

What are the benefits?

- No enrollment fee, monthly premiums, or deductibles. Most veterans have no out-of-pocket costs. Some veterans may have to pay small copayments for health care or prescription drugs.

- More than 1,700 places available to receive care. This means coverage can go with you if you travel or move.

- Fulfills the Affordable Care Act (ACA) requirement to have health care coverage.

Combat Veterans: If you served in a theater of combat operations after November 11, 1998, and were discharged on or after January 28, 2003, you have special eligibility to enroll in the VA health care system for 5 years from your date of discharge or release. The 5-year eligibility period begins on your discharge or separation date from active duty military service or, in the case of multiple call-ups, the most recent discharge date. National Guard and Reserve personnel who were activated and served in a theater of combat operations after November 11, 1998 may also be eligible for enhanced health care benefits.

For more information: **www.va.gov/healthbenefits/apply/returning_service-members.asp**

Apply: For more information about your health benefits, visit **www.va.gov/healthbenefits** or call toll free at: 1-877-222-VETS

Health insurance is expensive, but not having it can be financially devastating. Choose a plan—or a combination of plans—that makes sense for your unique situation.

TIP Confused yet? Here are three go-to resources that will help you figure out your health insurance options! www.healthcare.gov   www.statehealthfacts.org   www.healthinsuranceinfo.net

Visit **www.LifeDuringCollege.com** for more resources and exercises.

Paying for College

Depending on your COA, your FAFSA, your EFC (which will be noted on your SAR) and your enrollment status, you may qualify for a FSEOG or a Pell. Now, your FAA can tell you all about how your aid is disbursed, how interest will accrue, and if it is capitalized. For more information, check out the NSLDS.

So, you thought when you left the military that you also left behind a dictionary of acronyms? No such luck. Sometimes it feels like you need a degree just to figure out how to pay for college or understand the financial aid process. Thankfully, as a veteran, you are likely eligible for a combination of federal and state benefits that will offset the cost of attendance. In some cases, you may be eligible for a series of benefits and, if you intend to further your education beyond the baccalaureate level, it is imperative that you receive strong financial counseling to maximize your awards. Shortly after being admitted to your college, be sure to contact the office of financial aid and the veterans certifying official to discuss your individual situation.

In this chapter we will explain the most critical terms related to college finance, give you an overview of your options for paying for this investment that is your college education, and provide you with the websites and phone numbers that will be essential for figuring out your personal college financing plan. Here are the sections that will be included in this chapter:

- Independent status
- Work
- FAFSA
- Federal grants and work study
- Loans
- Veterans education benefits

Independent Status

For purposes of financial aid, a veteran is considered an independent, which is defined as a student who: (1) has engaged in active service in the U.S. Armed Forces (Army, Navy, Air Force, Marines, or Coast Guard), or has been a member of the National Guard or Reserves who was called to active duty for purposes other than training, or was a cadet or midshipman at one of the service academies, or attended a U.S. military academy preparatory school, and (2) was released under a condition other than dishonorable. As a veteran, you do not need to provide your parents' financial information on your FAFSA.

Work

While going to school full time and working is a challenge, it is not uncommon. In fact, nearly 39% of full-time college students work (Source: www.bls.gov). The benefits to working while attending school are

Consider This ...

29.6

(the average number of hours undergraduate students work* per week)

*includes work-study, assistantships, and traineeships

Source: US Dept. of Education Profile of Undergraduate Students, Sept. 2010
http://nces.ed.gov/

- a reduced debt load when you graduate

- work experience that can help you qualify for future internships and jobs

- experience managing time and balancing priorities

The drawbacks to working while in school are

- extra stress from trying to budget time and energy

- lack of focus on academics might mean less success in your classes

- little time for social or extracurricular activities

Even if you do decide to work while taking classes, you'll probably need to supplement your income with other sources. For many students, that means turning to Uncle Sam or private organizations for scholarships, grants, and loans.

The FAFSA

Completing the Free Application for Federal Student Aid (FAFSA) is a kind of rite of passage—for the student. As its name states, the application is free. It's also necessary if you want to be considered for the majority of financial aid options. Applications are accepted as early as January 1st and as late as the end of June, but you want to submit yours as soon as possible in order to have the best chance of receiving financial aid. Go to www.fafsa.ed.gov to complete yours online. Contact the Federal Student Aid Information Center at 1-800-4-FED-AID with questions you have about the form and/or the process.

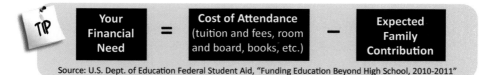

| Your Financial Need | = | Cost of Attendance (tuition and fees, room and board, books, etc.) | − | Expected Family Contribution |

Source: U.S. Dept. of Education Federal Student Aid, "Funding Education Beyond High School, 2010-2011"

After you complete your FAFSA, you will receive a Student Aid Report (SAR) that details your family's expected contributions to your college costs. Your eligibility for financial aid—and for different types of financial aid—will be determined based on this information.

Which EFC Formula Worksheet should be used?

There are three regular formulas and a simplified version of each:

- **Formula A** for dependent students

- **Formula B** for independent students without dependents other than a spouse

- **Formula C** for independent student with dependents other than a spouse

A Guide to Financial Aid Acronyms

Good To Know

COA:	Cost of Attendance
FAFSA:	Free Application for Federal Student Aid
EFC:	Expected Family Contribution
SAR:	Student Aid Report
FSEOG:	Federal Student Educational Opportunity Grant
FAA:	Financial Aid Administrator
NSLDS:	National Student Loan Data System
EEK:	The sound a student makes when he or she sees the total cost of textbooks for the semester

Federal Grants and Work-Study

Many schools participate in federal programs that offer aid in the form of federal grants and work study opportunities. Remember, you may be competing with other students for these grants and work study jobs, so fill out any required paperwork—including the FAFSA—as early as possible!

Federal Pell Grant: Students who demonstrate financial need may qualify for a Pell Grant. Pell Grants, which may be as large as $5,645, do not have to be repaid. If you are awarded a Pell Grant, your school may disburse the money to you directly or credit your account.

Federal Supplemental Educational Opportunity Grant: If you are awarded a Federal Supplemental Educational Opportunity Grant (FSEOG), you may receive up to $4,000 a year. The money will be disbursed to you by your college. You may receive checks or a credit to your account. You do not have to repay a FSEOG.

Federal Work Study: If you qualify for a work study program, you will be eligible for a job either on campus or with another organization that has an agreement with your college. You will be paid monthly wages by the college.

Teacher Education Assistance for College and Higher Education (TEACH) Grant: You may be eligible for up to $4,000 per year if you are enrolled in a teacher education program and agree to teach for a period of time in a high-need field or in a high-need school. If you complete your teacher education program but do not fulfill your contract agreements, you must repay the TEACH grant.

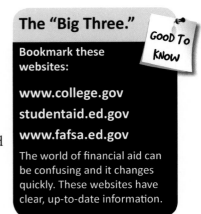

The "Big Three." *Good To Know*

Bookmark these websites:

www.college.gov
studentaid.ed.gov
www.fafsa.ed.gov

The world of financial aid can be confusing and it changes quickly. These websites have clear, up-to-date information.

Iraq and Afghanistan Service Grant: If your parent or guardian died serving in the military in Iraq or Afghanistan, you may be eligible for a federal grant up to $5,500.

Federally Funded Loans

There are a variety of loan options available to students. The following are the federally funded loan options:

Federal Perkins loans: Perkins loans are low-interest loans for students with exceptional financial needs. The U.S. Department of Education allots a certain amount to participating colleges, which determine the students with the greatest needs. Your college will either disburse Perkins money directly to you or it will credit your account. There are no fees for Perkins loans.

Good To Know According to the Consumer Financial Protection Bureau, "Ten percent of recent graduates of four-year colleges have monthly payments for all education loans in excess of 25% of their income."

Source: CFPB Report on Private Student Loans, 2012. Consumerfinance.gov

Subsidized (also known as the Federal Direct Stafford/Ford Loan): If the Department of Education determines that you have financial need, you may qualify for a subsidized loan, which means you will not be charged interest on the amount you borrow while you are enrolled (at least half time) in school. You will also get an interest-free grace period for the 6 months after you graduate, drop out, or drop below the minimum number of enrollment credits. If you apply for and receive a deferment after the grace period expires, you will not be charged interest while your loan is deferred.

Unsubsidized (also known as the Federal Direct Unsubsidized Stafford/Ford Loan): Same as above except Uncle Sam does not pay the interest on your loan while you're in school. You can wait to make payments until after you graduate, but the interest on your loan will accrue and be added to the total amount you owe when you do start making payments.

Private Student Loans

Private student loans are another option. Unlike the loans described in the above section, private student loans are funded by private institutions, such as banks and credit unions. While these loans are readily available for many borrowers, they carry more risk than those loans funded by the federal government. A private student loan may

Beware of scam artists who prey on students.

You should NEVER pay for scholarship information. There are no "exclusive" lists and opportunities that can be purchased. You should not have to give your credit card information in order to apply for a scholarship or grant.

- have a very high interest rate. We have seen rates as high as 18% for private student loans.
- have a variable interest rate. That means your monthly payment amount may change unexpectedly.
- require that you begin repaying while you're still in school.
- not offer loan forgiveness or forbearance.
- have a prepayment fee or penalty fees

A word of caution: Take your time to review all the options available to you. If you take out a loan it could be with you for many, many years. Spend some time calculating how long it will take you to repay the loans you take out (a simple financial aid calculator is available at **www.finaid.org**).

Other Options

There are many ways to piece together the funds you need to pay for your education. Here are some routes students take to make their college dream a reality:

State and local aid: Your state and local organizations may offer grants and scholarships. Go to the US Department of Education's Education Resource Organizations Directory website for all the links you need to find out about what aid your state and other organizations may have available.

Service: Students who serve in programs such as AmeriCorps may receive compensation and other benefits that will pay for some or all of their college costs or loans. Of course, serving in the military is another route to paying for one's education.

Scholarships: There are innumerable scholarships available to students—the key is to know where to look for them. Community and business organizations, unions, service clubs, and civic groups abound. Your parents' employers may have scholarships available, or the local Rotary Club, your honor society, your fraternity or sorority, your bank, an organization that focuses on your proposed area of study. Ask around, check your school's financial aid office, and use the Internet to search for scholarship and grant money.

Competitive or conditional grants: At **http://studentaid.ed.gov** you can find a list of grants for students with exceptional skills or who agree to "pay off" the grant with a term of service. For example, the TEACH Grant Program gives students money if they agree to teach for a certain amount of time in high-needs areas of the country. The Academic Competitiveness Grant is available to students who have proven themselves in a rigorous course of study.

Lower-cost education: Some students decide to lower the cost of their education in addition to finding ways to pay for it. For example, a student might take classes at the local community college during summer quarter.

Veterans Education Benefits

Many benefits are available to advance the education and skills of veterans that will ultimately support their career goals. Spouses and family members may also be eligible for education and training assistance. Some veterans find that they're eligible for more than one benefit or that one program is more suited to certain education and training goals than another. To learn about the various education and training programs administered by the Department of Veterans Affairs, we recommend that you begin your search by visiting the "Get Started" webpage: **www.benefits.va.gov/gibill/get_started.asp**

Post-9/11 GI Bill
www.benefits.va.gov/gibill/docs/pamphlets/ch33_pamphlet.pdf

The Post-9/11 GI Bill offers higher education and training benefits to Veterans, Service members, and their families who served after Sept. 10, 2001. If you have at least 90 days of aggregate active duty service after Sept. 10, 2001, and are still on active duty, or if you are an honorably discharged veteran or were discharged with a service-connected disability after 30 days, you may be eligible for this VA-administered program.

Montgomery GI Bill
www.benefits.va.gov/gibill/montgomery_bill.asp

The Montgomery GI Bill assists active duty and Reservists with the pursuit of higher education degrees, certificates, and other education and training.

Reserve Educational Assistance Program
www.benefits.va.gov/gibill/reap.asp

REAP provides educational assistance to members of the Reserve components called or ordered to active duty in response to a war or national emergency declared by the president or Congress.

Veterans Educational Assistance Program
www.benefits.va.gov/gibill/veap.asp

VEAP is available if you elected to make contributions from your military pay to participate in this education benefit program. The government matches your contributions on a 2-for-1 basis.

Survivors and Dependents Educational Assistance Program

www.benefits.va.gov/gibill/survivor_dependent_assistance.asp

The Dependents' Educational Assistance (DEA) program offers education and training opportunities to eligible dependents of Veterans who are permanently and totally disabled due to a service-related condition or of Veterans who died while on active duty or as a result of a service-related condition.

State Department of Veterans Affairs

www.va.gov/statedva.htm

After looking over the VA's website, be sure to visit your state's Department of Veterans Affairs webpage for state-specific benefits. The veterans certifying official at your college will assist you with determining the best way to use multiple federal and state benefits.

Paying for College **Exercises**

1. Visit the Department of Veterans Affairs Education & Training webpage: **www.benefits.va.gov/gibill/**. Look over the various benefits that you may be eligible for. Now visit your state's VA webpage and look over state-specific benefits. Make a list of questions for your college's financial aid office and veterans certifying official. Devise a plan of action.

2. Visit the "Big Three" websites on page 144 and explore the resources, tools, and documents that pertain to your financial situation. Write a review of the top 5 most helpful sections of these pages.

3. Make a list of organizations you and your parents belong to, interests you have, and subjects you would like to study. Search the U.S. Department of Education's Education Resource Organizations Directory website and/or your college's financial aid office for scholarship and grant opportunities that might be available to you based on your list.

4. Create a calendar for the upcoming year that will help you organize the various scholarship and aid deadlines.

Visit **www.LifeDuringCollege.com**
for more resources and exercises.

Budgeting Made Easy

CHAPTER 20

For many veterans, the transition out of the military entails learning how to make do with less once Uncle Sam no longer direct deposits a paycheck twice a month. This new way of living might precipitate comments like, "That's not in my budget" and "We're living a little lighter these days." The word budget might bring to mind restrictions and limitations, but a budget is simply a plan. Any limitations it involves are actually steps on the way toward a goal.

Budgeting when you're in college might seem unnecessary. After all, when you're broke, you're broke, right? What's to plan? When you're living on a monthly housing allowance from the Post-9/11 GI Bill and rummaging through your sea bag for MREs it may seem like making a budget is a frivolous exercise. But whether you're living on your own or if you're supporting a family, you need to budget, no matter if you make $1,000 or $100,000 a year. Don't stress: a budget doesn't have to take days to create. And while it may sound restricting, it can actually be quite freeing. A good budget, combined with savvy spending, will help you survive your college years in good financial shape.

This chapter will

- show you how to create a budget that works
- outline strategies for dealing with budget problems
- share tips for stretching your money

Create a Budget

A budget empowers you by giving you a true picture of your financial situation as well as a blueprint for making financial decisions. It's easy to think of things to want: a car, a vacation, graduate school. What's challenging is figuring out what actions you need to take now to be able to afford those things in the future.

Here's a simple approach to creating a budget that will work for you:

1. **Calculate your income.** How much money is coming in? Consider all sources, from scholarships, loans, grants, parents, jobs, investments, and savings.

Monthly Expenses FIXED	
Rent/Room Cost	$800
Meal plan	$300
Utilities	$100
Insurance	$60
Tuition	$1000
Auto payment	$350
Credit card payment	$80
Total FIXED Expenses	**$2,690**

Monthly Expenses VARIABLE	
Entertainment	$100
Transportation	$50
Clothing	$100
Eating Out	$75
Personal Care (haircuts, etc.)	$150
Gifts	$50
Other	$50
Total VARIABLE Expenses	**$575**

2. Calculate your expenses. How much money is going out? This step takes a little more time because you don't want to leave anything out and there are probably all sorts of expenses to consider.

Some expenses are **fixed**. In other words, they occur regularly and are usually in the same amount. Examples of fixed monthly expenses are things like rent, basic phone service, and car payments. Other fixed expenses occur quarterly or annually. Examples of these include tuition bills and auto insurance premiums.

Record your monthly fixed expenses. For annual or semi-annual expenses, record the cost per month (for example, if your auto insurance premium is $1,200 annually, write down $100 per month).

Other expenses are **variable**. This means that they vary from month to month and you have some control over how much you spend on them. For example, a person might spend $300 on food one month and $500 the next. One-time expenses are variable, as well.

So what amounts should you use for your variable expense categories? To construct a workable budget, you'll want to figure out your average monthly expenses. And, in order to get an accurate picture, you'll need to work with real numbers and keep a spending journal. Review your actual expenses from a two-month period and add up every latte, app, and shopping trip. If you use cash for most of your purchases, collect receipts or write down your expenses as you go through your day. For debit card purchases, you can use your bank statement to itemize your expenses.

Common Expense Categories

TIP

- **Housing**
- **Utilities**
- **Debt service** (i.e., anything you owe: car payments, credit card payments, etc.)
- **Insurance** (e.g., auto, health, renter's insurance)
- **Transportation** (e.g., auto repairs, bus fare, gas, tolls, registration fees)
- **Entertainment** (e.g., movies, eating out, Internet access, cable TV)
- **Personal** (e.g., food, clothing, health club fees)
- **Contributions** (to charities or other organizations)

3. Create an income statement.
Once you know your income and expenses, you can draft an income statement:

Monthly income − expenses (fixed and variable) = net income

An income statement will help you see your monthly bottom line. If your average income minus your average expenses equals an average negative balance, you know you'll need to make some adjustments: make more money or spend less.

Keep a Spending Journal

For 1 – 2 months, keep track of everything you spend. There are four common approaches to this mission. Try one or a combination of several:

Consider This ...

Keep every receipt and itemize your spending at the end of each day

OR

Carry a small notebook with you where you can note each expense

OR

If you use your debit card for most purchases, review your account records online at the end of each week and itemize expenses then.

OR

If you use your debit card for most purchases, review your transactions and itemize them using budgeting software (e.g., Quicken) or an online budgeting website such as www.mint.com

4. Make a plan.

After you've assessed your income and expenses as they are, you can make a plan for a financially sustainable lifestyle. Write down all of your fixed numbers—the income and expenses that can't or won't change in the near future. Then, take a second look at your variable expenses: Are there places you could nip and tuck that would leave your bank account looking better at the end of each month? Are there variable expenses that you haven't included that you need to plan for (example: gifts, spring break, or a bike tune up)?

> Creating a budget is not a one-time event. Review, reevaluate, and revise your budget regularly.

People who don't budget spend erratically—splurging here, denying themselves there—and feel anxious all the time because they don't know what to expect when they open their bank statement or bills. When you budget you can make rational decisions based on your plan. You might still be broke, but at least you'll be able to evaluate the situation wisely. You might even decide to change your fixed expenses by, say, renting a cheaper place or selling your car.

Tips for Stretching Your Money

Here are some time-tested tips for surviving on a student budget:

Use coupons. If you're going to buy something, you might as well spend a little time to get the best deal. Retailers make this easy for you by sending coupons in the mail or posting store circulars near the entrance of the store. The Web makes it even easier with coupon purveyors such as Groupon (**www.groupon.com**) sending targeted advertising and deals to consumers.

Shop sales. Just about everything goes on sale eventually. When you see something you want, watch and wait for it to go on sale. You can also ask a salesperson when the item is likely to go on sale so that you'll know when to beeline it to the store. Some grocery stores have select times of the month for reduced prices. Once you know what those days are, you can plan your major grocery trips accordingly.

Comparison shop. It takes more time, but when you want or need to make a purchase it's worth checking out your options. Look for store circulars, browse the aisles, and use the Internet to find out who is offering the lowest price and best deal on the things you want.

Ask for a deal. Sometimes all you have to do is ask. Call your credit card company and ask for a lower interest rate or to have a fee waived. Ask a salesclerk if you can get the sale price now or if you can at least hold the item until the sale.

Find freebies. College is full of freebies if you know where to look. You can snack on samples at local grocery stores, find promotional gifts, and attend company-sponsored free events. Warning: This becomes a lifetime habit. We know many people who decades out of college still perk up at the mention of free samples!

Flash your student or military ID. Many businesses offer discounts to students and current members of the military, including Reservists and National Guard members. Don't be shy to ask about a student or military discount and always carry your IDs with you, just in case.

Spend to save. Sometimes you have to spend money to save money. For example, spending $30 every three months to change your car's oil is costly—but not as much as having to replace your car's engine when it runs out of oil and burns up.

Live simply. Reconsider all the things you "need" to have. Cable television, a gym membership, new books…you might surprise yourself with how well you adapt to life without these "necessities."

Wait before you buy. Impulse shopping can blast a good budget to shreds. Resolve to wait 48 hours before making a purchase of something you want but don't need. If, after 48 hours, you still feel you can't live without it, figure out how to pay for it and make the purchase. You'll find that you end up making purchases that you truly appreciate and don't regret.

Lower credit card rates if you're activated. Called to active duty? Under the Servicemembers Civil Relief Act, existing law limits to 6 percent interest on credit obligations incurred prior to military service or activation, including credit card debt. For more information: **www.justice.gov/crt/spec_topics/ military/scratext.pdf**

Budgeting Made Easy **Exercises**

1. Keep a spending journal. For one week, write down every penny you spend and categorize each item you buy. Write a one-page reflection on what you learned about your spending habits.

2. Review your fixed expenses. Are there ways to reduce any of them? How would you go about reducing some of your fixed expenses? What would you sacrifice? What would you gain?

3. Review your variable expenses. Which categories cost you the most each month? How would you go about reducing some of your variable expenses? What would you sacrifice? What would you gain?

4. Research the best deals for college students in your community and present your findings to the class. You may choose to focus on a theme—for example, *Cheap Eats* or *Entertainment.*

Visit **www.LifeDuringCollege.com**
for more resources and exercises.

Banking

CHAPTER 21

They come bearing gifts of free t-shirts and water bottles. Sometimes they even offer gift cards or cash. While your piggy bank sat mutely in the corner of your room, these banks send cheerful representatives to campus to sign you up for a new checking account. You need a bank, they need customers. It's a win, win situation, right?

Right. Except that banks are in the business of making money and you'll want to make sure the bank you choose doesn't make too much money off of you. Consider this: the average checking account costs over $200 annually. Free checking is no exception, as the fees for ATM and teller use, automatic bill payment, check writing, and overdrafts mount up. We know one college student who was shocked when she added up all the fees she had paid over a one year period—and realized it was over $800!

Avoiding such financial disasters doesn't mean you have to keep your money tucked away in a box under your bed; you just need to choose—and use—your checking account wisely.

This chapter will

- help you choose a bank that makes sense for you
- teach you how to keep track of your account balance
- offer you money-saving tips for using banking services
- discuss military banking options

Choosing a Bank

You have three main choices: a bank with physical locations, an online bank, or a credit union. Banks and credit unions offer similar services, but differ in whom they serve and how they do business. Banks want to make a profit, and do so by charging service fees and offering low interest rates on deposits. Credit unions, on the other hand, are nonprofit and are owned by the members they serve. Their business model allows them to offer services at a much lower cost and to provide higher rates on deposits. However, credit unions are not open to everybody, they usually have a limited number of branches and a smaller network of ATMs, and they tend to offer a limited range of services. If you are eligible to join a credit union, it may be a good choice for you, but make sure you consider all potential costs before you make a decision.

Traditional banks with physical branches are the most common choice for students. There might even be bank branches on your college campus. Most traditional banks will offer a student checking account that has low to no monthly maintenance fees. They count on the fact that college students will rack up fees that offset the free checking. (Every bank has different fees, but some common ones to be aware of include fees for dipping below the minimum monthly balance, bouncing a check, or using a non-affiliated ATM.) Traditional banks generally have online banking services so you can do most of your banking from the comfort of home.

Online banks are another option. They usually offer free or low-cost checking accounts and services, and may have better interest rates than traditional banks. Some even offer no-fee ATM use at any ATM, which can be a bonus when you're out on the town or when you travel home for breaks. They have fees for overdrafts and non-sufficient funds and the like, of course. One downside of choosing an online bank is that it may be inconvenient to make deposits. You may have to set up automatic deposits or send the checks to them in the mail, though some banks offer convenient at-home deposit options where you can submit a deposit using your smartphone.

Evaluate your banking needs before you make a decision. Review your previous banking habits, as well as your current situation. Consider where you will live throughout the year and what kind of banking you think you will need. Be realistic about your banking habits and needs. (You've got enough to do just figuring out new classes.)

Your Banking Needs	
How many checks will I need to write a month?	
How many ATM withdrawals will I want to make per month?	
What kind of minimum monthly balance—if any—can I count on maintaining?	
What are my online banking needs and preferences?	
Do I ever overdraw my account?	
Do I want to earn interest on my deposits?	
Will my primary banking be done online or at the bank branch?	
Do I tend to keep track of my account balance?	
Will other people, such as my parents or spouse, be making deposits into the account? How can I make it easy for them to do so?	

Visit **www.LifeDuringCollege.com**
for more resources and exercises.

Once you figure out how you're likely to use a checking account, consider the options available to you. Here are some items you can evaluate in order to comparison shop:

- ➤ Interest rates
- ➤ Online banking features
- ➤ Number and location of ATMs
- ➤ ATM fees
- ➤ Deposit options
- ➤ Loan services
- ➤ Credit card/Debit card services
- ➤ Bill pay options

- ➤ Federal Deposit Insurance
- ➤ Fees and requirements
- ➤ Alerts and protection against fraud
- ➤ Money market accounts
- ➤ Convenience of locations
- ➤ Overdraft protection
- ➤ Brokerage services
- ➤ Reward points for credit card or debit card use

Before you sign up with a bank, find out how other people will be able to make deposits into your account and what kind of information those other people will need in order to do so. Many students will receive at least periodic monetary assistance from parents and other people, so it makes sense to choose a bank account that makes it easy for them to make deposits.

Keep Track of Your Account

If someone offered to pay you $200 to balance their accounts correctly, would you do it? When you balance your own account and avoid costly mistakes like overdrafts and additional fees, you get to keep more of your money. Here are some ways to manage your account without making it a full-time job:

- Keep track of debit card purchases and ATM transactions in a register

- Use duplicate checks so you have copies for your reference

- Note when you make deposits and when the funds will be available

- Keep receipts for purchases, withdrawals, and deposits

- Establish a regular time each week to review your accounts and update any activities you may have forgotten

- Set up your online banking so you can check your account balances and recent activity

It's important to check your account balance regularly. Doing so will help you avoid any surprises that can crop up, such as an overdrawn account or a faulty deposit.

Tips to Help You Save

Know what part of "free" means "fee." Sure, your bank will charge fees for some services. If you know what they are you can avoid getting stuck paying for them.

Use direct deposit. Many banks will waive certain fees if you use direct deposit. If your employers offer direct deposit, sign up for it.

Maintain a minimum balance. Banks calculate your minimum balance in one of two ways: daily minimum balance, which requires you to maintain the balance every single day, and average daily balance, which requires you to maintain the balance as an average over the billing cycle. Make sure you choose a realistic balance option—if you have a choice between the two—and maintain the balance required by your bank.

Opt in for overdraft protection. Sometimes things happen that are beyond your control. For example, you might write a series of checks and then realize your student loan funds were never deposited. With overdraft protection, banks advance you the money to cover the checks you have written. There are usually fees for this service. Know what your bank's policies and procedures are and how much overdrafts might end up costing you.

Ask for discounts and waived fees. Once your bank has you as a customer, they want to keep you. Don't be shy about asking your bank for a better deal or to waive certain fees.

Be smart about using services:

- *Know where your bank's no-fee ATMs are located.* If you use ATMs that are not part of your bank's system, you will be charged an average of $2.40 per transaction, according to Bankrate.com's most recent survey of checking accounts. Often, you will be charged twice: once by your bank and again by the ATM company.

- *Request cash when you use your debit card to make purchases.* Most banks don't charge fees for "cash back" transactions.

- *Limit transactions and bank visits* if your checking account has a maximum number of such services allowed per month. However, it's important to note that there are so many banking options available that you shouldn't have to settle for a bank that limits transactions and bank visits.

Don't order checks from your bank. Most banks charge between $12 and $17 for a box of 250 checks. A cheaper option is to order checks directly from the check-printing company. Find these companies online.

Use online bill pay options. You'll save on stamps and checks. Also, you can set up automatic payments so you won't get stuck paying the fees vendors charge for late payments.

Military Banking Options

As a veteran you have several banking options available with perks such as free checking, competitive rates for auto and home loans, and no fee ATMs. A few options to explore include:

- USAA
  www.usaa.com

- Navy Federal Credit Union
  www.navyfederal.org

- Wells Fargo Military Banking
  www.wellsfargo.com/military

- Bank of America Military Banking
  www.bankofamerica.com/military-banking/overview.go

- PNC Military Banking
  www.pnc.com/en/personal-banking/banking/military-banking.html

Banking **Exercises**

1. Fill out the chart on p. 154, then compare three specific banking options available to you. Which option do you think will be the best fit for your banking needs and habits?

2. Research online money tracking sites that can help you manage your account. Some of them categorize expenses, send alerts when funds are low, and help you visualize your cash flow with charts and graphs. Your bank probably offers such online services. If they don't, research online or check out money tracking apps like Mint, Spendee, and BUDGT.

3. Make a banking action plan and post it where you'll remember to follow it. Your action plan might include a schedule for bill paying and balancing your checking account, a method for keeping track of receipts and transactions, and ways to leverage your bank use (for instance, can you pay for your tuition with a debit card that earns you airline miles?).

Visit **www.LifeDuringCollege.com**
for more resources and exercises.

Your Credit

CHAPTER 22

Somewhere, even as you read this, your life is being summarized as a series of entries about what you owe, what you buy, and how timely you pay your bills. Every time you do something to affect your credit—sign up for a new credit card, make a late payment, complete a loan application—it is recorded in a report that may be read by future lenders, landlords, and even employers.

Why is everyone so interested in your credit report? What does it reveal about you? Think of it as a credit report card that provides a snapshot of your financial responsibility. It's a record of every time you apply for or accept a loan or other form of credit. It also tracks how you use your credit—how much you have available, how much you owe, and how you repay. The people who will be considering granting you a student loan or giving you a new credit card want to know your financial track record.

Do you know what your credit report contains? If not, you should. Even if you haven't used credit much at this point in your life, you need to be watchful to make sure someone else isn't using it for you.

This chapter will tell you what you need to know about credit. We will

- explain what a credit report is
- outline the importance of credit reports
- tell you how to obtain a free copy of your credit report
- describe how to maintain good credit

What is a Credit Report?

A credit report is a detailed history of your borrowing habits for the past seven to ten years. It's a record of what you owe and to whom, what you've paid, and if you've made any late payments. It also reveals personal information, such as your social security number, current and former addresses and telephone numbers. Any time you order a report or authorize someone else to do so, the inquiry is recorded. Several companies called credit bureaus compile and maintain databases for the purpose of creating such reports.

According to federal law, credit bureaus are allowed to give your credit report to the following parties:

- Creditors who are considering giving you credit

- Employers considering you for employment, promotion, reassignment, or retention

- Insurers considering you for an insurance policy or reviewing an existing policy

- Government agencies reviewing your financial status or government benefits

- Anyone with a legitimate business need for the information, such as a potential landlord

- Parties who have a court order or federal jury subpoena for your credit report

- A third party to whom you have requested, in writing, that your credit report be issued

There are two kinds of inquiries made regarding your credit. **"Hard" inquiries** are when you seek to obtain credit or when you authorize someone access to your full credit report. **"Soft" inquiries** are requests for general information rather than a full credit history. Examples of soft inquiries include when you request a copy of your own credit report and when a company is gathering marketing information about potential customers.

Why is My Credit Important?

Your credit report and credit score might seem irrelevant at this point in your life, but they are very important. Good credit opens doors and lowers rates. Here are just a few things credit can affect:

Insurance rates. Many insurance companies use credit scores to decide whether to offer a customer car insurance and how much to charge him or her for it.

Your ability to secure a loan. If your credit score indicates you are a credit risk, you may be denied credit.

Credit Report vs. Credit Score

GOOD To KNOW

Credit Report: A detailed record of what you owe and to whom, what you've paid, if you've made any late payments, and where you've lived.

Credit Score: A shorthand way for a lender to tell if you're a good credit risk or not. A high score means you're a lower risk and have a better chance of obtaining credit at better interest rates. While each credit bureau has its own system, they all take into account the following factors: your ability to make payments on time, the amount of credit you owe, the type of credit you owe, the length of your credit history (the longer the better), and the number of requests for new credit.

Interest rates on loans and credit. People with a good credit history get better interest rates and more credit made available to them. For example, someone with an excellent FICO (Fair Isaac Corporation, one of the major credit score reporting agencies) credit score (720 – 850) might be able to secure a 36 month auto loan at an interest rate of 4.953%. Someone with a fair FICO score (660 – 689) would qualify for an auto loan at a much higher interest rate, say 8.347%. The difference in monthly payments on a $10,000 car would be $16, or over $570 over the life of the loan. On larger loans the difference is even more significant, of course. Someone with an excellent credit score might pay as much as $4,800 less on a $100,000 30-year fixed mortgage than someone with merely a good credit score. The short story: People with the best credit scores pay less interest. (Check out **www.myfico.com** for credit score/loan amount calculators.)

Employment. Some employers use credit history to assess a job applicant's responsibility and reliability. If an employer or potential employer denies you employment, a promotion, or security clearance because of your credit history, they are required by law to let you know and to give you time to review your report and respond.

Your ability to rent an apartment. Landlords want to know if their potential tenants are likely to pay rent on time. People with better credit scores may be more likely to secure a rental unit—and less likely to pay a huge deposit.

Get Your Free Credit Report

The Fair Credit Reporting Act requires each of the nationwide consumer reporting companies (Equifax, Experian, and TransUnion) to provide you with a free copy of your credit report, at your request, once every 12 months. You need to be proactive with your credit. Check it now and address any problems immediately.

Conventional wisdom says it takes years to remove a blemish from a credit report, but seconds to put one on. Checking your credit report on a regular basis will enable you to monitor and prevent any illegal use of your credit.

> **Get Your Free Credit Report Now!** TIP
>
> **www.annualcreditreport.com**
> **877-322-8228**
>
> The three major credit bureaus (Equifax, Experian, and TransUnion) are required by federal law to give consumers one FREE credit report each year. When you go to their websites you might find other services for sale. Don't worry about that stuff yet. Just get the free report.

GOOD TO KNOW — Ordering a credit report DOES NOT affect your credit score.

Applying for a credit card DOES affect your credit score.

Maintain Good Credit

Avoiding credit cards might make good financial sense, but it doesn't help you build credit. The best thing to do at this point in your financial life is to obtain credit, use it, and pay it off. That way you'll have a solid history for future lenders to review—and you'll be more likely to get the mortgage or business loan you want in the future.

Even responsible people can end up with dings on their credit report. Here's how to keep your report nice and shiny:

Building good credit is simple:

Consider This ...

1) Get credit
2) Use it
3) Pay it off
While it's smart to be cautious with credit card use, don't make the mistake of not getting a credit card or never using the ones you have. Credit agencies want to see you have a history of good credit use.

Know what you owe, know who you owe, and pay your bills on time.

When you move, make sure every business you deal with has your change of address on file. You don't want to miss a payment because the vendor is sending bills to an old residence!

Set up a folder in your email account for e-bills, as they can easily get buried in the inbox.

Don't miss a payment. Remember: Inadvertently missing a payment—even missing one payment because of the vendor's mistake—can cause as much headache as blatantly ignoring a due date.

Repairing your credit is another challenge, but it's a process worth starting now if your credit report is less than stellar. Here are some ways to repair your credit effective immediately:

Set up a system today for paying all current bills on time.

If you have big outstanding balances that you can't pay off, contact the business to see if they'll negotiate a payment plan with you. Vendors lose a lot of money when they send accounts to collections agencies, so they'll probably be willing to work with you.

> Vendors recoup pennies on the dollar when they send accounts to collections. They usually prefer to work with customers and arrange a payment plan rather than go through collections.

GOOD TO KNOW

If you see an error on your credit report, document it right away. Write a letter to the credit bureau explaining your dispute, send in any information that substantiates your claim, and request that the error be corrected. Inform the creditor as well. Remember to make copies of all related paperwork and keep careful records.

TIP

Need help repairing your credit? Your first stop should be the Federal Trade Commission website at **www.ftc.gov.** Beware of credit repair scams!

Your Credit **Exercises**

1. You probably saw this one coming: Check your credit report now. Go to **www.annualcreditreport.com** and request a free credit report. Review it. If there are any errors, address them as soon as possible.

2. At this point in your life, do you need to build, maintain, or repair your credit? Decide on two action steps you can do this week to improve your credit. Tell a partner what your action steps are, then report back to him or her when you've completed them.

3. If you were an employer, would you want to know the credit histories of your prospective employees? Explain. Do you think it is right for an employer to have access to this information?

4. Debt accumulation among college students is at an all-time high. Do you think policies or required programs should be put into place to correct this situation? If so, why? If not, what do you think would help improve the situation?

Visit **www.LifeDuringCollege.com** for more resources and exercises.

Credit Cards & Debt Management

CHAPTER 23

The Freshman 15 is nothing. Let's talk about the Senior 30,000. We're not talking pounds here, of course, but dollars in debt. Debt is money owed to a creditor. According to Sallie Mae and the U.S. Department of Education National Center for Education Statistics, the average undergraduate college student graduates with over $28,400 in student loan debt and over $3,000 in credit card debt. Yikes! To make matters worse, veterans tend to have more debt than average Americans.

The college years are not just about personal growth, it turns out. They're also about credit, debt, and other financial management topics. And you'll want to get financially savvy now or you could end up graduating with a diploma and a mountain of debt.

On a brighter note, as a veteran, you are also likely to have a generous benefits package to finance your education. In other words, with careful planning and discipline you do not have to join the ranks of students who are inordinately burdened by debt. While your circumstances may require you to accumulate some debt during your college years, you can do so wisely. This chapter will show you how by

- helping you understand debt
- recommending strategies to keep your debt in check
- teaching you how to recognize if your debt is out of control
- outlining your options if your debt becomes overwhelming

Understanding Debt

If you have debt, you are not alone in your age group. Recent statistics illustrate the reality of undergraduate student loan and credit card debt:

- In 2013, 70% of college students graduated with student loan debt.
  (source: projectsonstudentdebt.org)
- From 2008 to 2012, average student loan debt increased 6% per year.
  (source: projectsonstudentdebt.org)

- 1 in 10 students graduate with over $40,000 in student loans. (source: projectsonstudentdebt.org)

- Undergraduate students' average monthly credit card balance is over $3,000. (source: Sallie Mae)

- Almost 7% of debtors applying for bankruptcy are between the ages of 18 and 24. (source: Government Accountability Office)

While these figures may seem alarming, it's important to recognize that not all debt is bad.

Good Debt vs. Bad Debt

Good debt is debt that allows you to access something of long-term value, such as an education or a home. Bad debt is the result of short-term, "feel-good" decisions, such as purchasing something you can't really afford and don't really need.

Student loans that help further your education will probably pay off in nonmaterial as well as material ways. Statistically, people with post-secondary degrees do much better in the job market than those who don't have them. Because of the importance of a college education, student loans are generally viewed as low-interest, high return investments. Much like home loans, they promise higher future income. Also, both of these types of debts offer tax advantages—you can write off a portion of the interest, which pulls down the cost of the debt itself.

> **Consider This ...**
>
> **55%** of students who took out loans for their education feel burdened by their debt.
>
> **54%** of student borrowers said they'd take out less in loans if they had to do it all over again.
>
> **70%** of student borrowers said student loans were worth incurring for personal growth.
>
> Source: Nellie Mae 2002 National Student Loan Survey.

> **Good To Know**
>
> Let's say you charge $2,000 on a credit card to cover part of your tuition one semester. If that credit card company charges 19% interest and you make the minimum monthly payments, it will take you over 8 years and almost another $2,000 in interest to pay off that charge.
>
> Source: Government Accountability Office.

Credit card debt can be in both categories. It's good in that accumulating some debt and paying it off is necessary for establishing good credit. It's also good because it's convenient and secure. You're not likely to rush to the airlines to pay for a flight with a wad of cash; you're even less likely to call the bank to put a stop payment on the cash someone lifted from your wallet. Credit cards allow you to book flights and hotels, they provide extra insurance for some purchases, and they tend to be much better than cash when you travel and want to get the best exchange rate. Credit cards can be stolen, but they're usually protected. This means you probably won't be responsible for charges racked up illegally with your card.

But the praise stops there. Credit card debt can be very bad. Interest rates that begin as low, introductory rates quickly become unmanageably high. When you can't pay more than the minimum monthly payment, you end up paying doubly and even triply for that cool gear you bought five years ago. How bad is credit card debt? It depends on how much you owe. How long will it take you to pay the debt down? How high is the interest rate? Is it limiting other opportunities, like your ability to apply for another type of loan? The answers to these questions will tell you if your credit card load has moved from bad to ugly.

According to student loan lender Sallie Mae, student credit card use has increased. In 2009,

1 in 3 students reported putting tuition on plastic.

9 in 10 students reported charging textbooks and other direct education expenses to their cards.

Consider This ...

Keeping Debt in Check

In the whirl of classes, financial aid paperwork, and new freedoms, many students quickly lose track of what they owe and to whom. Be aware of for-profit companies that prey on people who feel overwhelmed by debt. You should not have to pay anyone to manage your debt situation; there's plenty you can do on your own and if you feel really buried there are well-respected nonprofit organizations, like Consumer Credit Counseling, that can help you. Here's how to get a handle on your debt:

Step 1: Figure out what you owe. Pull out your latest credit card and student loan statements and create a table of the following: the amount you owe to each vendor, the interest rates, and your minimum monthly payments. (Note: Go to **www.nslds.ed.gov**, the National Student Loan Data System website, to see all of your student loans in one handy place.) Your student loan payments won't begin until you graduate, but it's good to keep track of them starting now.

Debt Record					
Name of loan	Principal owed	Interest rate	Annual interest payment (est.)	Minimum monthly payment	Goal monthly payment
BankTwo Visa	$5,522	15.75%	$5,522 X 0.1575 = $870	$65	$150
Fuel Card	$648	11.25%	$648 X 0.1125 = $73	$20	$80

Step 2: Prioritize pay offs. You need to make the minimum monthly payments on all debts or your credit score will suffer. But creditors' required minimum monthly payments are designed to pad their pockets and raid yours, so do all you can to pay more than the minimum. Pay off higher interest loans first. If Card A has an 18% interest rate and Card B has a 9% interest rate, pay the minimum on B and pay off A as quickly as possible.

Step 3: Consolidate debt. You don't need to do this "officially," using a for-profit company to manage your accounts. You can usually take care of this step on your own. For example, pull all your credit card debt onto one low-interest card. It will lower your overall interest payments and allow you to pay one bill instead of several, thereby increasing the odds of paying the bill on time and keeping your credit score up. Caution: Do not use your new card to charge items or you'll likely end up with more debt than when you started the transfer process.

Step 4: Live within your means. Stop all impulse buying and cut corners where you can. Pack food with you to class so you won't be tempted by the campus eateries. When a new gadget or item catches your eye, give yourself a cool-off period of at least 48 hours to consider the pros and cons of purchasing it. It can be empowering to say no to such purchases, especially when you realize how doing so will benefit your future.

Step 5: Stay focused. Keep your debt and your financial priorities in view. Review your statements and always know how much you owe and how much you can handle. The students who end up buried by debt are usually shocked when they realize how much they've racked up. Don't let unnecessary debt sneak up on you.

Debt Record					
Name of loan	Principal owed	Interest rate	Annual interest payment (est.)	Minimum monthly payment	Goal monthly payment

Visit **www.LifeDuringCollege.com** for more resources and exercises.

Is Your Debt Out of Control?

If any of these statements describe you, your debt has moved into the driver's seat:

_____ I shop impulsively, buying things I don't really need.

_____ I make late or minimum monthly payments.

_____ I have credit cards that are at, or close to, my credit limit.

_____ I'm not sure how much I really owe.

_____ I use cash advances to pay my bills.

_____ I've had my credit card declined.

_____ My family members or friends are concerned about my spending habits.

If you recognize yourself in these statements, you can take action now to take back control. Here are a couple of options:

Contact a counselor at the Consumer Credit Counseling Service (www.cccsstl.org) or the National Foundation for Credit Counseling (www.nfcc.org). Both are nonprofit organizations that offer education and credit counseling. There are plenty of unethical credit counseling services, so make sure you stick to these two respected ones.

Contact your creditors. Call your current credit card companies and ask them to lower the interest rates. Creditors often want to work with their customers. After all, they want their money. If you can't pay them they'll end up having to send your account to collections, which means a big loss for them.

If one or more of your creditors has turned your account over to a collection agency, you need to know the following:

- A collection agency may contact you by phone, e-mail, mail, or in person.
- They cannot call your employer or members of your family.
- No one else can be forced to pay a debt that is yours alone.
- You can get them to stop calling you by sending them a letter. They are then only allowed to contact you regarding plans to bring legal action against you.
- You do not need to tolerate rude or belittling remarks.
- Collection agencies are not empowered to work out terms of payment.
- If you think you are being treated unfairly, contact the FTC at (877) FTC-HELP or go to **www.ftc.gov**.

Credit Cards & Debt Management **Exercises**

1. Fill out the table ("Debt Record") on page 166. How long will it take you to pay off your current bad debt? The National Foundation for Credit Counseling website (**www.nfcc.org**) has a great calculator that can help you answer this question.

2. Tour the websites of both major credit counseling services: Consumer Credit Counseling Service (**www.cccsstl.org**) and the National Foundation for Credit Counseling (**www.nfcc.org**). Which sections of the two websites do you find most helpful and interesting? What facts, tips, and strategies did you learn that you will likely use?

3. Develop a plan for keeping your debt load as low as possible. How can you limit spending now so that you're not paying for it well into the future? Remember to keep your goals in plain sight—literally, write them where you can see them on a regular basis.

Visit **www.LifeDuringCollege.com**
for more resources and exercises.

Vital Skills

CHAPTER 24

You've shown your capacity to do something unique and adventurous through your military service. Maybe you experienced multiple deployments and interacted with remote cultures. Or perhaps you coordinated search and rescue missions that saved lives. You already have a broad understanding of the world; now is the time to acquire new knowledge and build a fulfilling life.

Whether you graduate with a degree in Engineering or a degree in Comparative Literature, there are certain fundamental skills and qualities to develop during your college years. Who do you want to be when you graduate? What do you want to do? Where do you want to go? Keep these questions in mind as you work toward your degree, and remember, like the military, your upcoming college years are a transformative time that will lead you toward becoming a more powerful and well-rounded person. Use this time wisely to get involved, to be inquisitive, and to take risks. And, be sure to develop the vital skills that stand out to employers.

Your future employers have clear ideas of what they want from you and other college graduates. While employers expect students to graduate with in-depth knowledge of their field, they value broader skills and characteristics as well. For example, a 21st century graduate needs to know how to organize and interpret information and how to work in a diverse team, whether he/she is a medical researcher or an advertising executive. If your future employer is yourself, you have even more reason to develop a wide range of skills.

Must-have Skills and Traits

The Association of American Colleges and Universities released a report in 2013 that outlined the results of an employer survey conducted by Hart Research Associates about what college graduates need to know and be able to do when they enter the workforce. What may be surprising to some people is that the good old-fashioned liberal arts education is increasingly more valued. The pace of change in today's workplace is so fast that employers care less about a person's specialized skills and more about how innovative and adaptive he or she is. The computer language you learn in 2015 might be obsolete in 2020, but your willingness to learn a new computer language and your ability to work well with a team will keep *you* on the cutting edge.

Here is what you need to get out of college:

Relevant Experience
Challenge yourself with extracurricular activities. Take on internships and field projects. Look for ways to apply your knowledge to real-world situations. Not only will that experience make your résumé stand out, it will also make your college years more interesting and fulfilling.

Communication Skills
Strong written and oral communication skills are essential whether you become an engineer, a teacher, or an entrepreneur. Take classes that challenge you to communicate effectively in a variety of modes. If you hate public speaking, now is a great time to face that fear. Take an introductory communication class or join an organization such as Toastmasters.

Critical Thinking
Critical thinking is analyzing and interpreting information, synthesizing ideas, and reflecting on what you know. Ideally, every class will encourage and develop your critical thinking skills. You can hone your critical thinking by stepping outside your "comfort zone" and questioning your assumptions and knowledge. Take classes in a variety of subjects, attend lectures on topics outside your discipline, and seek out friends and classmates who offer diverse opinions.

Research and Information Literacy
One challenge of living in the 21st century is the barrage of information available at a keystroke. To be successful you need to learn to find and evaluate sources, organize information, and understand statistics.

Teamwork
What you learned in preschool is more important than ever: It turns out that sharing, taking turns, listening, working together and respecting others is not only essential for building a Lego® town. It's also essential for working in most organizations in the 21st century. Experience working with teams of people from diverse backgrounds is especially valuable, as the workforce today is incredibly diverse and fluid.

Leadership
Leadership is a difficult skill to identify and quantify, but it's valuable nonetheless. Take on leadership roles in your sport, clubs, activities, and projects that you do while you're in school so you'll gain experience and confidence.

Flexibility
A job candidate who demonstrates the willingness and ability to adapt to change, respect for differences and diversity, and an interest in developing skills and experience is very attractive to potential employers. If you're flexible, you'll also be more likely to stay interested and engaged in your work. A few ways to develop this skill are to complete coursework outside of your major; participate

in a variety of activities, including volunteering and part-time employment; and study abroad or learn a new language.

Civic Knowledge and Participation

There are dozens of metaphors for the modern world: It's flat, it's shrinking, it's a global village. Whatever you call it, you will be expected to understand political, social, and economic conflicts and issues more than previous generations did. Employers depend on educated, civically-involved employees to run their organizations and companies.

Character

In many ways, employers care more about who you are than what you can do. Are you loyal, responsible, honest, respectful, creative, resourceful, kind? All of these traits are markers of good character and, while they don't show up on your transcript, you can demonstrate them in other ways. Your references and documentation of involvement in certain projects and extracurricular activities may help you establish your good character.

Vital Skills **Exercises**

1. Use the table on the following page to consider each of the nine skills and traits described in this chapter, document your accomplishments, and set short-term (this year) and long-term (by graduation) goals.

2. Consider the classes you are currently enrolled in. How can you maximize your experience in those classes to develop the vital skills and traits covered in this chapter?

3. Which extracurricular activities are you currently involved with? Choose two of the vital skills and traits discussed in this chapter and create a plan for developing them further through your participation in extracurricular activities.

Visit **www.LifeDuringCollege.com**
for more resources and exercises.

Vital Skills & Traits	Accomplishments	Short-term Goals	Long-term Goals
Relevant Experience			
Communication Skills			
Critical Thinking			
Research and Information Literacy			
Teamwork			
Leadership			
Flexibility			
Civic Knowledge and Participation			
Character			

Visit **www.LifeDuringCollege.com** for more resources and exercises.

Educational Employment & Your New Career

CHAPTER 25

Most veterans have little exposure to the private sector prior to joining the military. Additionally, with a few exceptions, the only schools and education they've experienced have been directly tied to their Military Occupational Specialty (MOS) or their unit's training requirements. The resulting lack of civilian work experience and limited postsecondary education creates one of the largest obstacles for veterans during their transition out of the military.

As a first-year student you might be so busy figuring out your new environment and managing your academic load that the idea of preparing for a job after graduation seems ambitious to say the least. And it is ambitious. However, after you've settled into your new life, set aside some time to learn about ways of getting "relevant experience" while you're in college.

Educational employment can help you gain experience while you're pursuing your degree. The most common kind of educational employment is the internship, but there are many other options available, including part-time jobs, volunteering, externships, and work study. All educational employment is valuable: it adds to your experience and confidence, bolsters your resume, and positions you to find a job right out of school. In fact, according to the National Association of Colleges and Employers, students with internships are more likely to be offered a job upon graduation and more likely to be offered a higher salary than their counterparts who did not do internships.

You already possess a vast amount of practical experience, discipline and "real world" knowledge. But assembling all this into action points and further building on these strengths is part of your mission as a student as is locating the resources and allies that will play an integral role in the process. To support you with this endeavor, this chapter will

- provide an overview of the different types of educational employment available

- recommend ways to find educational employment opportunities

- discuss the benefits of networking

- give tips on finding a good fit with educational employment
- address how to translate your military experiences into civilian language
- highlight veteran-specific resources

Research Careers of Interest

Pop quiz. What does being a student and looking for a job have in common? They both require extensive research. Throughout your years in college, part of your research should include forecasting the job market to see which fields are in high demand and which ones are saturated. To support your career investigation, consider starting with the U.S. Department of Labor's Bureau of Labor Statistics. Their Occupational Outlook Handbook provides comprehensive information concerning the projected needs of various occupations as well as required training and median pay. Knowing the requirements and anticipated openings of your field of interest will assist with strategically mapping out things like internships, certificates, workshops and other career-related items: **www.bls.gov/ooh/**

Types of Educational Employment

Sure, you want to have a knock-out resume when you hit the workforce as a new graduate. But educational employment is about more than adding bullet points to the "relevant experience" section of those job applications. It's also about learning what interests you and what your strengths and weaknesses are. The most valuable aspect of some internships is that they teach you the ins and outs of a particular field—and sometimes you learn that you don't actually *want* a future in that field. You can get some amazing hands-on experience while you're in school. Here are some of the options:

Internships
Internships are short-term employment assignments during which you receive valuable hands-on training and experience in a career. Some internships last a college term, while others may be a year long or take place during summer break. Some colleges actually coordinate internships for students, placing students with a particular company or organization and awarding college credit for the completed internship. Usually you have to pay tuition for this kind of internship and you may have to complete a project at the end of the experience. Other internships are an agreement between the organization and the student. Students do not receive any college credit for these kinds of internships and do not have to pay any tuition. Some internships are paid positions.

Cooperative Education
Similar to internships, cooperative education programs give students a chance to apply their college learning by working in their chosen field. The student, college, and company/organization agree on the scope of the work the student will do. Often, students get paid for their cooperative education work. They also have course work and classes associated with their work experience.

Externship

An externship is a mini-internship. During an externship a student spends a brief period of time, perhaps a day or a week, following an employee of a business or organization through his or her workday. Externships give students a quick view of a career and the types of tasks and challenges one encounters on a daily basis in that career. Many college students complete externships during school breaks.

Volunteering

Many college students volunteer because they enjoy it and they are committed to supporting a worthy cause. Volunteering can also be a great way to get hands-on experience in the field of your choice. For example, if you are interested in working in education, you might volunteer for an after-school program or as a tutor. If you are interested in pursuing a medical career, volunteering at a hospital or medical clinic would be fulfilling and give you valuable real-world training.

Summer and Part-time Jobs

Most college students work at some point during the year, so it makes sense to choose jobs that give you experience in your chosen field. Lifeguarding may be fun and active, but working for a local law firm would be more valuable for a student interested in pursuing a law degree.

Work Study

You may be able to find valuable work experience without ever leaving campus. Many colleges offer work study programs in which students work in order to subsidize their tuition and other expenses. Talk with your advisor and your school's employment office to see if there are opportunities that would be relevant to your career choice. For example, if you are thinking about a career in science, perhaps there is a lab assistant position available in your school's science department. Also, be sure to check with your Veterans Certifying Official as there may be positions available to work with veterans on campus, such as through Financial Aid or the Veterans Office. For more information on the Department of Veterans Affairs Work Study program and for an application, see **www.vba.va.gov/pubs/forms/VBA-22-8691-ARE.pdf**

Finding Educational Employment Opportunities

Your college probably offers all sorts of educational employment opportunities, both on campus and with companies and organizations that have developed relationships with the college. However, such positions can be quite competitive and hard to come by. Oftentimes, to secure the perfect educational employment, you will have to do your own legwork. Here's how:

Get to Know Your Instructors

College instructors often have the best information about internships and other opportunities because they have established relationships with business owners and leaders in the community. Ask your instructors if they know of any opportunities they would recommend.

Visit the Career Center

Your campus career center is not just for post-graduation job opportunities. In fact, it's a good idea to visit the career center early in your first year, as it will probably have resources to help you map out your major and career plans. It's the go-to place to find out about internships, events, workshops, career fairs, and employer information sessions. Many career centers also provide mock interviews along with guidance on how to write an effective resume.

Check the Alumni Center

Your college alumni center probably maintains a database of alumni with information about their professions. See if your alumni center will furnish you with a list of alumni who work in your desired career and who might be willing to speak with you about opportunities. Even if the alumni you talk with don't end up knowing of an appropriate educational employment opportunity for you, they would probably be willing to give you recommendations or advice.

Pick Up the Phone

Find local business and organizations relevant to your career choice. Research the ones that most interest you, then call their human resources department to ask if there are any educational employment opportunities available.

Check Professional and Trade Associations

Professional associations and clubs often help their member businesses and organizations find quality candidates for internships, volunteer positions, and part-time work listings. Even if the association does not currently have a lead on an educational employment opportunity, it might give you contact information for a company that does.

Check the Veterans Office

Many employers looking to hire veterans or offer internship opportunities will contact both the Career Center and Veterans Office. Some job announcements may also be posted in a Veterans Lounge or on a school's Student Veterans of America Facebook page. Check with your college's Veterans Certifying Official and SVA chapter for more information.

Network

As is the case with post-college employment, networking is essential to finding a position. Talk with family, friends, and contacts who might have a connection—or who might know someone who has a connection—to the industry or organization you're trying to break into.

More on Networking

The role of networking can't be overstated when we talk about locating opportunities and jobs. At this point in your life you don't necessarily need a lot of high-powered contacts. Just take time to connect with people—instructors, other students, community members. Your network is simply all the people you know. In college you will probably expand your network exponentially. Connecting with others will make your college years more interesting and fulfilling. Your network will also be a means to find out information (about great restaurants, the best mechanics, and job opportunities, for instance) and to get your name out.

Now is a good time to reflect on your use of social media, which can be a great way to network—or can lead to a complete disaster. Assume professors and potential employers will be able to see everything on your Facebook page; "privacy" settings do not guarantee you privacy, and plenty of people have found out the hard way that employers and colleges can gain access fairly easily. Make sure the image you're projecting online isn't detrimental to your current reputation or future prospects.

Finding a Good Fit

Your time is at a premium and the last thing you want to do is to commit to something that ends up being a worthless experience. Sure, you can expect some drudgery in an internship or cooperative education job, but it should also help you hone your skills and expand your understanding of the field. Before you accept an educational employment position, ask yourself these key questions:

- Will this position help me develop the skills and experience I will need to land the job I want after college?

- Do I fully understand the job description and expectations? Can I fulfill them?

- What kinds of projects will I be working on? What have previous students worked on and what were their results?

- What have other students experienced in this company or organization?

- What kind of compensation will I be receiving? If it's not financial, will I be receiving educational credit or valuable work experience?

- What kinds of expenses might I incur if I accept this position? Will I need to pay for transportation costs? Will I need to get a new wardrobe?

Translate Your Military Experience into Civilian Language

"Served as an 11B team leader and completed two deployments in support of OEF and OIF. Supervised and drafted EERs for seven E4s and two E3s. Conducted monthly PMCS on 5 vehicles worth an estimated $700K. Honorable discharge." This all sounds good, right? Well, that depends on your audience.

As a veteran the use of acronyms is second nature. However, to a potential employer this type of resume will need to be accompanied with a manual to decipher the code and figure out what exactly it is you're talking about. To ensure that all your hard work in the military is accounted for, it is

TIP

MILITARY.COM VETERANS SKILLS TRANSLATOR:

www.military.com/veteran-jobs/skills-translator

This handy tool translates your military experience into civilian skills!

imperative that you keep your prospective employer in mind when writing your resume. Keep the language simple and approach it from a civilian's perspective. Thankfully, with more veterans returning to school, many career centers have a designated staff or at least an employee who has received specialized training and is familiar with veterans' unique experiences. This person can also provide a fresh pair of eyes to ensure that you effectively capture your strengths in ways that are easy to understand.

Veteran-Specific Resources

An added benefit of being a veteran is that there are many non-profit, county, state and federal offices in addition to community-based organizations such as the VFW and American Legion that want to see you succeed. Although this list is not exhaustive, it provides several starting points to assist with your job search. Be sure to check with your college's Veterans Office and other student veterans for more recommendations.

Career One Stop: **www.careeronestop.org**

Military One Source: **www.militaryonesource.mil**

U.S. Department of Labor Veterans' Employment and Training Service (VETS): **www.dol.gov/vets**

Troops to Teachers: **www.troopstoteachers.net**

Helmets to Hardhats: **www.helmetstohardhats.org**

And don't forget – as a veteran, you will also receive "Veterans' Preference" with some employers, which mean additional points will be added to your application. For more information, check out Feds Hire Veterans: **www.fedshirevets.gov/job/vetpref/**

Educational Employment **Exercises**

1. Visit your college's career services center and the alumni office—or their web pages—to locate internship and other educational employment opportunities. Which postings most interest you?

2. Discuss educational employment opportunities with your advisor: What types of placements have other students received? What kinds of positions would he/she recommend for you? What kinds of prerequisites are there for getting the kinds of placements you would like?

3. Research businesses and organizations in your community that you might be able to volunteer for or intern with in the future. What are their requirements or expectations for volunteers and interns?

Visit **www.LifeDuringCollege.com**
for more resources and exercises.

Life During College Sources

Chapter 4

Baum, Ph.D., Katrina, Shannon Catalano, Ph.D., Michael Rand, and Kristina Rose. "Stalking Victimiza-tion." *USDOJ: Office on Violence Against Women*. Web. 26 Oct. 2010. <http://www.ovw.usdoj.gov/>.

"College Drinking: A Snapshot of Annual High-Risk College Drinking Consequences." *Research about Alcohol and College Drinking Prevention*. National Institute of Alcohol Abuse and Alcoholism, 1 July 2010. Web. 31 Dec. 2010. <http://www.collegedrinkingprevention.gov/StatsSummaries/snapshot.aspx>.

Sampson, Rana. "Acquaintance Rape of College Students." *COPS Community Oriented Policing Service*. U.S. Department of Justice. Web. 28 June 2010. <http://www.cops.usdoj.gov/>.

"Seven Tips for Campus Safety." *Security On Campus, Inc.* Web. 01 Jan. 2011. <http://www.securityon-campus.org/index.php?option=com_content&view=article&id=1563>.

"The Campus Safety and Security Data Analysis Cutting Tool." *Ope.ed.gov*. U.S. Department of Education Office of Postsecondary Education, 2010. Web. 28 June 2010. <http://ope.ed.gov/security/>.

Chapter 6

Park, Kang H., and Peter M. Kerr. "Determinants of Academic Performance: A Multinomial Logit Approach." *Journal of Economic Education* Spring (1990): 101-11.

"Class Attendance." *Minnesota State University Mankato*. Web. 26 Oct. 2010. <http://www.mnsu.edu/cetl/teachingresources/articles/classattendance.html>.

Chapter 7

Coffey, Heather. "Experiential Education." *LEARN NC*. Web. 01 Sept. 2010. <http://www.learnnc.org/lp/pages/4967>.

"David A. Kolb on Experiential Learning." *Contents @ the Informal Education Homepage*. Web. 02 Jan. 2011. <http://www.infed.org/biblio/b-explrn.htm>.

Fisher, Alec. "Critical Thinking: An Introduction." Cambridge University Press, 2001. Web. 9 Sept. 2010. <http://catdir.loc.gov/catdir/samples/cam031/2002265188.pdf>.

Watson Glaser Critical Thinking Appraisal: WGCTA. --. Harcourt Brace World, 1964. Print.

Chapter 8

Boyd, Robyrne. "Do People Only Use 10 Percent Of Their Brains?: Scientific American." *Science News, Articles and Information | Scientific American*. Web. 05 Oct. 2010. <http://www.scientificamerican.com/article.cfm?id=people-only-use-10-percent-of-brain>.

Chudler, Eric H. "Neuroscience For Kids - Explore the Nervous System." *UW Faculty Web Server*. Web. 02 Jan. 2011. <http://faculty.washington.edu/chudler/introb.html>.

"Does Multitasking Lead To A More Productive Brain? : NPR." *NPR : National Public Radio : News & Analysis, World, US, Music & Arts : NPR*. Web. 02 Aug. 2010. <http://www.npr.org/templates/story/story.php?storyId=127771658>.

Hallowell, Edward M. *CrazyBusy: Overstretched, Overbooked, and about to Snap : Strategies for Coping in a World Gone ADD*. New York: Ballantine, 2006. Print.

Merlo, Carol. "Too Much to Do and Not Enough Time: The Liability of Multi-Tasking." *ArticlesBase.com*. Web. 02 July 2010. <http://www.articlesbase.com/self-help-articles/too-much-to-do-and-not-enough-time-the-liability-of-multitasking-924021.html#ixzz0udU45pE4>.

"THE BRAIN FROM TOP TO BOTTOM." *LE CERVEAU À TOUS LES NIVEAUX!* Web. 02 Jan. 2011. <http://thebrain.mcgill.ca/flash/i/i_07/i_07_p/i_07_p_tra/i_07_p_tra.html>.

Chapter 9

«Study Skills Resources.» *Cornell Learning Strategies Center*. Web. 02 Jan. 2011. <http://lsc.sas.cornell.edu/>.

"Toastmasters International - Visual Aids & PowerPoint." *Toastmasters International - Home*. Web. 02 Jan. 2011. <http://www.toastmasters.org/MainMenuCategories/FreeResources/NeedHelpGivingaSpeech/BusinessPresentations/VisualAidsPowerPoint.aspx>.

"Where To Study / How To Study." *Dartmouth College*. Web. 01 Aug. 2011. <http://www.dartmouth.edu/~acskills/success/study.html>.

Chapter 10

"Academic Honesty : Center for Academic Support." *University of Rochester*. 3 Sept. 2010. Web. 29 Dec. 2010. <http://www.rochester.edu/college/ccas/AdviserHandbook/AcadHonesty.html>.

Argetsinger, Amy. "Technology Exposes Cheating at U-Va." *Washingtonpost.com*. Web. 12 Sept. 2010. <http://www.washingtonpost.com/ac2/wp-dyn?pagename=article&node=&contentId=A638-2001May8>.

"Character Traits Associated with the Five Dimensions of Character and Social Responsibility." *Association of American Colleges and Universities*. Web. 29 Dec. 2010. <http://www.aacu.org/core_commitments>.

Definition of Plagiarism. "Glossary." *The United States Department of Justice*. Web. 29 Dec. 2010. <http://www.justice.gov/criminal/cybercrime/cyberethics_glossary.htm>.

Gabriel, Trip. "Plagiarism Lines Blur for Students in Digital Age." *The New York Times* 1 Aug. 2010, A1 sec. Web. 30 Sept. 2010. <www.nytimes.com>.

"Fundamental Values Project." *Center for Academic Integrity*. Web. 15 Sept. 2010. <http://www.academicintegrity.org/fundamental_values_project/>.

Chapter 11

Greenberger, Dennis, and Christine A. Padesky. *Mind over Mood: Change How You Feel by Changing the Way You Think*. New York: Guilford, 1995. Print.

Chapter 13

Bandura, A. "Self Efficacy." *Encyclopedia of Human Behavior*. Ed. V.S. Ramachaudran. 1994. Print.

Cloud, John. «Yes, I Suck: Self-Help Through Negative Thinking - TIME.» *Www.time.com*. Web. 11 Aug. 2010. <http://www.time.com/time/health/article/0,8599,1909019,00.html>.

Diversity of College Students: The Latest Research." *DiversityWeb - A Resource Hub for Higher Education*. Web. 02 Jan. 2011. <http://www.diversityweb.org/research_and_trends/research_evaluation_impact/benefits_of_diversity/impact_of_diversity.cfm>.

Payán, Rose M., and Michael T. Nettles. "Current State of English-Language Learners in the U.S. K-12 Student Population." *ETS Home*. Web. 5 Dec. 2010. <http://www.ets.org/>.

"Positive Attitude Delays Aging." *BBC News - Home*. Web. 02 Jan. 2011. <http://news.bbc.co.uk/2/hi/health/3642356.stm>.

Chapter 15

ACSM. Web. 02 Jan. 2011. <http://www.acsm.org/>.

Diagnostic and Statistical Manual of Mental Disorders: DSM-III-R. Washington, DC: American Psychiatric Association, 1994. Print.

Parker-Pope, Tara. "Gene Mutation Tied to Needing Less Sleep." *The New York Times.* 14 Aug. 2009. Web.

"What Happens When You Sleep?" *National Sleep Foundation - Information on Sleep Health and Safety | Information on Sleep Health and Safety.* Web. 24 Oct. 2010. <http://www.sleepfoundation.org/article/how-sleep-works/what-happens-when-you-sleep>.

Chapter 18

National Association of Insurance Commissioners (NAIC). Web. 1 Oct. 2010. <http://www.naic.org/>.

Chapter 19

Federal Student Aid - Information on Grants, Student Loans, Scholarships and Other Financial Aid. Web. 1 Aug. 2010. <http://federalstudentaid.ed.gov/>.

"Funding Education Beyond High School 2010 - 2011." *Student Aid on the Web.* Web. 15 Aug. 2010. <http://studentaid.ed.gov/>.

College, Education, Financial Aid Info. Web. 21 Dec. 2013. <http://www.college.gov/>.

FAFSA on the Web-Federal Student Aid. Web. 21 Dec. 2013. <http://www.fafsa.ed.gov/>.

Chapter 20

«Checking Study: A Detailed Look at the Results.» *Bankrate.com.* Web. 02 Jan. 2011. <http://www.bankrate.com/brm/news/chk/chkstudy/20060417b2.asp>.

U.S. PIRG. Web. 02 Jan. 2011. <http://www.pirg.org/>.